By the same author:

The Dictionary of Palmistry

Letter Writing Improved.

PALMISTRY MADE EASY

Palmistry for Vocational Guidance

By

JAGAT S. BRIGHT

JAICO PUBLISHING HOUSE

Mumbai ● Delhi ● Bangalore
Calcutta ● Hyderabad ● Chennai

PALMISTRY MADE EASY
ISBN 81-7224-225-5

First Jaico Impression : 1965
Second Jaico Impression : 1970
Third Jaico Impression : 1975
Fourth Jaico Impression : 1983
Fifth Jaico Impression : 1993
Sixth Jaico Impression : 1996
Seventh Jaico Impression : 1998

Published by:
Ashwin J. Shah
Jaico Publishing House
121, Mahatma Gandhi Road
Mumbai - 400 001.

Printed by:
R.N. Kothari
Sanman & Co.
113, Shivshakti Ind. Estate,
Marol Naka, Andheri (E),
Mumbai - 400 059.

PREFACE

"This man is a palmist!"

This silly bit of news went round like wildfire in a marriage party in New Delhi last week, and soon I was mobbed by men, women and children, who rose from their dining chairs, leaving the eatables uneaten, and came forward thrusting their hands, as if they wanted to get rid of these clumsy instruments, or these were mirrors in which they wanted me to see the picture of their future!

Well, well, well! Palmistry indeed is a photo of your future but it has to be formed dot by dot like a radio-photo transmitted over long distances across oceans and mountains. From mounts and lines, from dots and dashes, from stars and stripes, the palmist proceeds to construct the three-dimensional picture of your character and career, your past, present and future.

It is the success of my book DICTIONARY OF PALMISTRY which has received unprecedented warmth of a response that has encouraged me to undertake more pioneering work along scientific lines in the woods and jungles of what Palmistry at present is.

This work deals with Palmistry in a methodical and scientific way for the benefit of the young students and those who are on the look out for a career suited to their talents and tempers.

There are two kinds of men in the world: those who collect money to do the work, and those who do the work to collect money. To the latter class belong most of us —men and mice, ministers and menials. Great men like Mahatma Gandhi, and even Henry Ford, belonged to the former class. Henry Ford treated money like just another "raw material" to keep his factories going, and this is how and why he became a billionaire! "He never seemed to have any money on him. Never gave money a thought, he'd say, ignoring the wince of a visitor who might be wondering from where the next payment on the mortgage was coming. Money had come to mean to Ford precisely what his coal heaps and scrap piles meant —material to keep the plant running." Yet he was a man who could buy a continent or run a sub-express to Calais! "He was broke again when the government issued a commemorative stamp in honour of Thomas Alva Edison, and Ford attended the ceremonies at Atlantic City incident to the first-day sale of the new postage. A two-column cut of Ford buying the first stamp carried lines which said he had to borrow two pennies from Mr. Russo, the mayor, to make a purchase."

So money is a way of life. Do not make it a way of death. Your work is more important than your money. Do not make money you get more important than the work you give. That way lies your death, your disaster, your doomsday.

With this book in your hand, you can follow the highways in your hand, head and heart to the homeland of your health and happiness.

Bon voyage!

J. S. B.

"Premrose",
V-278, Rajouri Gardens,
New Delhi-15.
October 25, 1963.

THE GREATEST TRUTH
> may lie in smallest things

THE GREATEST GOOD
> in what we most despise,

THE GREATEST LIGHT
> may break from darkest skies,

THE GREATEST CHORD
> from even the weakest strings.

—**CHEIRO**

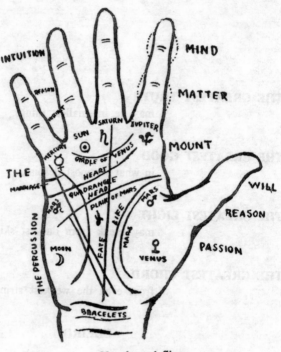

Number of Signs

CONTENTS

CONTENTS

Chapter One

MODERN PALMISTRY

Yes, palmistry is a thing you can play at or work at.
I worked at it as seriously as I worked at my B.A. degree,
which I sandwiched in between two seasons of hand-reading.
You may feel that I am shooting a line about this B.A.
business; in these days, when showmen so often claim bogus
degrees, I expect my qualification to be suspected. But any
one who cares to look in the Manchester University Calen-
dar for the list of graduates will find my Honours Degree
mentioned. I do not think my degree in English is a
marvellous achievement—but it is not a lie. So please for-
give my mention of it.

—Dennis Barry Jackson, B.A
"The Modern Palmist", page 12.

The palmists are becoming highly educated; and the
highly educated people are becoming palmists. It is no
longer a science that belongs to the gypsies. It is no longer
a message of the mountebanks. It is now being reduced
to a science. It has become a systematised knowledge
that you can pursue with pleasure and profit.

Palmistry is no longer a profession of the beggars. A
palmist is no longer a spiv lurking for mugs—to fleece
the fools "by offering the future for a florin". Both the
palmists and the palmistry-hunters are highly educated
people. They are seriously devoted to this science. If
this were not a science, they would not have been so
seriously devoting all their lives. As Mr. Jackson puts it:

A good palmist can really bring about a great
deal of good. Like the teacher or the priest or the
doctor he can give advice. The advice of the

teacher or the priest or the doctor is often forgotten, but the advice of the palmist is remembered. Believe me, this is true! I have been a teacher, and much that I taught was quickly forgotten, if I heard at all, for I argued for hours at a time, and my audience received all my erudition free of charge. But when I was a palmist and people queued up and paid five shillings for a five-minute interview, they hung upon every word, as though I were a Delphic oracle.

I

ANCIENT AND MODERN

Palmistry is at once the most ancient and the most modern science. 'If you are suspicious, throw away your suspicion. If you are superstitious, throw away your superstition. Bring with you an open and scientific mind.' The wisdom of the past must be coupled with the scientific methods of the present to bring out the best in palmistry. You have to study the following aspects of the hand before arriving at a final verdict:—

1. General shape of the hand.
2. Size of the hand.
3. General character of lines.
4. Specific character of lines.
5. The texture of the hand.
6. The colour of the hand.
7. The mobility of the hand.
8. The suppleness of the hand.
9. General shape of the palm.
10. Fine markings of lines.
11. Mounts on the hand.

12. Wetness or dryness of hand.
13. The length of fingers.
14. The length of phalanges of fingers.
15. The character of fingers.
16. The character of the thumb.
17. The shape of nails.
18. The colour of nails.
19. Spaces between fingers.
20. General impression.

All these factors should be kept in view and considered before pronouncing the judgment.

II

THE LINEAR CHARACTER

The Empty Hand

The hand which displays only the important lines and nothing of the subsidiary lines is called an Empty Hand. There is no network of fine lines on this hand. The possessor of such a hand is free from nervous excitement. He is a practical man of the world, and not a high-strung person incapable of living with anybody. The Empty Hand forgets and forgives easily and quickly. He does not brood over grievances and complaints long. He does not feel things deeply. He does not dwell over the past. He is plain and straightforward. He is slow but strong. He possesses directness of character. He loves discipline and method. He makes a good scientist. He is hard-working and active mentally and physically.

The Full Hand

A palm fretted with a network of lines shows a confused mind and high-strung mentality. The owner is worried with or without reason, in and out of season. Worry is his both virtue and vice. It springs from his deep imagination. He is unpredictable. He is vividly imaginative, artistic and creative. He can become a good scholar, poet, artist, musician. He has vitality and brilliance. But due to his confused outlook he can seldom bring out the best in him. He shirks responsibility. "He is good in examination but shy in class-work". He lives dramatically on a tight-rope. His life is exciting but not happy.

The Golden Mean

The golden mean is a hand neither very empty nor very full. It combines the best qualities of the both and defects of the neither. The average hand is neither very full nor very empty. That is the hand of the very practical common man who lives his life instead of roaming in a dreamland.

III

THUMB AND HANDS

A general shape of thumb and hands give a clue to the inner nature of man. Thus Mr. Jackson has it:

'I must agree that habitual gestures do shed light upon character—Sir Winston Churchill's habit of sticking his thumbs aggressively forward out of his pockets is a characteristic denoting the leader or man of action; little men demonstrate with their hands to make up for lack of inches; nervous people wring their hands; actors display character by the simplest hand-movements; painters of old masters take enormous pains over the position and shape of hands, and so on.'

IV

THE ADMINISTRATIVE HAND

Those who are ambitious to become administrators, join Indian Administrative Service, Indian Foreign Service, Indian Audit and Accounts Service, should look out for appropriate signs on their hands.

A strong vertical Line of Fate is the signal point for high administrative ability. The student should have an "advanced" hand. A simple elementary hand is not the right kind of hand for a successful administrator.

Whorl-type fingerprints are also a good sign.

The first finger is usually larger than the third in a great administrator.

The hand should be of the "Empty" kind. A "Full" hand shows sensitivity and this is not a good characteristic for public relationships. A "Full Hand" shirks responsibility and so seldom will such a person try for I.A.S. And if he does, he will give up midway!

"The hand of the administrator should be large, healthy and lined by the four main lines well developed, and few minor lines. The lines of head should dip slightly or fork at the end."

BIG BUSINESS BOSS

A big Business Boss has characteristics of an administrator. Besides, he has a plump hand with a prominent
Mount of Venus. The fingerprints are whorls, showing
financial acumen. The Fate Line is clear and long. The
Head Line is horizontal.

WISE WELFARE WORKER

The hands of a successful welfare worker are plump.
Fingers have thick lower phalanges. It has a Line
of Sympathy.

SPORTS WORLD

The hand of a sportsman is rather elementary. A good
Fate Line indicates skill and body control.

ACTOR'S HAND

The Line of Head is broad. It carries straight across
the hand, then twists unexpectedly towards the end.

Madame Sarah Bernhardt's hand had a twin Fate Line.
The hand was distinguished and usual.

A good actor has a whorl on the tip of the ring finger.
The hand is very sensitive and impressionable. The little
finger reaches high beyond the top knuckle of the long
ring finger. The Head Line is sloping.

INFANTRYMAN

"The hand of the good infantry man will have a short,
rather horizontal Head Line, showing a strong natural
conventional intelligence. This will not be 'tied' to the
Life Line, for the best soldiers are not cautious. That
is why they are often dead."

LITERARY MAN

A literary man has an advanced sensitive hand. His fingers turn inwards. The little finger, though long, bends towards the ring finger. The Line of Head dips very low. A whorl on the third finger and a long little finger are signs of expressive ability.

SCIENCE OF EXPERIENCE

Palmistry is the science of experience. Only by experience, study, insight and hard work one is able to diagnose one's character properly.

> 'It is fascinating to weigh up a complete hand. Contradictory features can be most puzzling, but most intriguing. In the end it is only experience and observation which count. Nobody can become a complete palmist simply by reading books, no more than anyone can become a Shakespeare by learning how to parse a sentence. Palmistry, like any other art, has to be studied.'

Chapter Two

THE SCIENTIFIC BASIS OF PALMISTRY

Cheiro learned the science of palmistry at the foot of the Himalayas—and from a Hindu guru! He predicted the partition of India about twenty years before the actual event.

—Subhash J. Rele
in the "Sunday Standard"

In his famous book **World Predictions** published in 1928, Cheiro (the pen-name of Louis Hammon) wrote: "England will give India her freedom but religious warfare will rend that country from end to end, until it becomes equally divided between the Mohammedans and the followers of Budha and Brahma."

But Cheiro's predictions about India were based on a knowledge he acquired in India. His father had destined him for priestcraft, but he was too adventurous to be churchillian, and disregarding his parents' advice, he sailed to see the world. He landed in Bombay and travelled north. For more than two years he lived at the foot of the Himalayas as the devoted disciple of an Indian Yogi. It was here that he learnt the ancient Hindu science of Palmistry.

It is written in the Vedas, according to W. O. Judge, that "Knowledge travels from East to West and from West to East again." According to occultists, all the scientific knowledge which now we find in the West, not only Palmistry, but also physical sciences, including Atomic Energy and Theory of Relativity, has travelled from East to West, and now it is returning home from West to East.

Even a die-hard materialist like Henry Ford believed that he and his contemporaries were not the first in the department of automobile engineering. He felt that all he was doing he had already done it in previous ages!

According to William C. Richards, the author of **The Last Billionaire: Henry Ford** (page 300) "He told associates he felt there was nothing in the world he had not seen in a previous life and also that work would be futile if it was impossible for man to use the experience collected in one life in the next."

I

ANCIENT WISDOM

Palmistry embodies the most ancient wisdom of the world. **The Old Testament,** one of the oldest living books, has it: "And God made marks upon the hands of men that the sons of men might know them." Alexander the Great, who bore the brunt of brilliant battles all his life and cannot be accused of superstitious sentimentalism, said about Palmistry: "The study is worth the while of an elevating and inquiring mind."

An Indian Science

That Palmistry is an Indian science, Cheiro acknowledges in his book **Language of the Hand:**

"To consider the origin of this science, we must take our thoughts back to the earliest days of the world's history, and furthermore to the consideration of a people the oldest of all, yet one that has survived the fall of empires, nations and dynasties, and who

are today as characteristic and as full of individuality
as they were when thousands of years ago the first
records of history were written.

"I allude to those children of the East, the Hindus,
a people whose philosophy and wisdom are everyday
being more and more revived. Looking back to the
earliest days of history of the known world, we find
that the first linguistic records belong to the people
under consideration, and date back to the far distant cycle of time known as the Aryan civilization.

"Beyond history we cannot go, but the monuments
and cave temples of India, according to the testimony
of archeologists, all point to a time so far beyond the
scant history at our disposal that in the examination
of such matters our greatest knowledge is dwarfed
into infantile nothingness........."

Written on Human Skin!

There exists in India an extremely ancient book on
Palmistry, jealously guarded in one of the ancient cave
temples, which Cheiro claims to have seen:

"This book was of human skin, pieced and put
together in the most ingenious manner. It was of
enormous size and contained hundreds of well-drawn
illustrations, with records of how, when and where
this or that mark was proved correct.

"One of the strangest features in connection with
it was that it was written in some red liquid which
age has failed to spoil or fade. The effect of those
vivid red letters on the pages of dull yellow skin was
most remarkable. By some compound probably made
of herbs, each page was glazed, as it were by varnish;
but whatever the compound may have been, it seemed
to defy time, as the outer covers alone showed the
signs of wear and tear. As regards the antiquity of
the book there coul'; be no question. It was apparent-

ly written in three sections or divisions, the first part belonged to the earliest language of the land, and dated so far back that very few of the Brahmins even could read or decipher it.   There are many such treasures in Hindustan but all are so jealously guarded by the Brahmins that neither money, art, nor power will ever release such pledges of the past."

II

MODERN SCIENCE

Beyond Indologists and Egyptologists and Biblical authoritarians ("What evil is in my hand?—Sam XXVI, 18; "Length of days are in her right hand, riches and honour in her left"—Proverbs III, 16; "And receive his mark in his forehead or in his hand"—Revelation XIV, 9) there is the evidence of modern scientists and the modern scientific method behind the truth of Palmistry as a working science.

Balzac, the great novelist, who was a keen observer, although not actually a scientist (But what is science without keen observation?   "Science is the systematic classification of experience"—George Henry Lewes) wrote in Le Cousin Pons:—

"To learn to know the disposition, in the atmospheric variations of the hand, is a more certain study than that of physiognomy.

"Thus, in arming yourself with this science, you arm yourself with a great power, and you will have a thread that will guide you into the labyrinth of the most impenetrable hearts.

"To predict to a man the events of his life by the sight of his hand is not more extraordinary to him who has received the power of knowing it, than to say to a soldier that he will fight; a barrister that he will speak; or a shoemaker that he will make a pair or boots.

"The line where flesh ends and nail begins, contains the inexplicable mystery of the constant transformation of fluids into horn, showing that nothing is impossible to the wonderful modification of the human substance.

"Well, if God has printed to the eye of certain clear-seeing minds, the destiny of each man, on his physiognomy—taking this word as meaning the total expression of the body—why should not the hand give the characteristics of the physiognomy, since the hand contains the whole of the human acting and its only medium of manifestation?"

Diagnosis of Disease

The possibility of fingerprints being used to help diagnose disease has been discussed in the London magazine **Prediction.** The article is based on the researches carried out by the Superintendent F. R. Cherill, the Scotland Yard fingerprint expert, and three London doctors. The author, Miss Vera Compton, writes:—

"Periodic scrutiny of the finger imprints of a person suffering from spinal tuberculosis showed that with the progress of the disease, the skin ridges had atrophied to knife-edged dimensions. The white lines on the finger-tip imprints continue to be shown after death.

"Mr. Cherill and his collaborators feel that a prolonged scientific analysis would, in some cases, supply evidence of incipient disease and of its progress."

Post-Mortem Effects

Of post-mortem effects, Miss Vera Compton writes:—

"Mr. Cherill found, as a result of examination of the hands of decomposing corpses over a long period, that as a rule the muscles and skin of the left hand of the cadaver exhibit signs of greater decomposition than the right hand. He suggests that a possible explanation is that the muscles, tendons and neurones are usually less developed in the left hand than in the right, and consequently putrefy more readily after death.

"Since the left hand appears to be more susceptible to post-mortem changes than the right, Mr. Cherill thought the left hand of a living person might show certain signs indicative of disease or that the signs might even precede the approach of disease in some instances. This appears to be in fact the case.

"The markings studied by Mr. Cherill appear on the finger-tip imprints (which, of course, are negative) as white lines of characteristic appearance. The lines are not of occupational origin, since they are often found on the hands of babies, and are indicative neither of youth nor of age, because they are found on the hands of persons of all ages. Whatever the origin of these lines, they are apparently indicative of certain pathological conditions, present and future."

Change of Lines

So the scientists have after all come to believe that lines on the hands are not entirely meaningless! As doctors, they are more interested in diseases than in health and happiness. But these lines cannot be one-side picture only. If some lines indicate disease, there must be other lines whic indicate health. And this is exactly what the Palmistry believes! Besides, these lines change, as the subject passes from disease to health or vice verse. And here we have the evidence of palmists who have made a scientific study of Palmistry. Thus Alice Denton Jennings says in **Your Hand Tells All:**

> "The lines of the hand change only under the influence of the mind, the will, the emotions and particularly under the deep-reaching influence of disease. It is these impressions which result in the birth of the little accessory lines that attach themselves to the main lines, bar or impede them, as well as form figures of varicus kinds......crosses, triangles, dots, islands, etc. The shape of the hand never changes."

Chapter Three

CAREERS AND COURSES

The hand is the organ of organs, the active agent of the passive powers of the entire system.

—Aristotle

One of the most important Hindu sayings is: "Five fingers in a hand are not equal." As all the fingers of a hand are not equal, so all the members of a family cannot have the same fate and fortune. All brothers and sisters have different destinies.

If a father is successful, it does not mean that his son will be equally prosperous. The son may have quite a different destiny. Therefore, a father has to watch the career of every child individually. And here Palmistry plays a great role. If one were versed in the laws of Palmistry, he can easily guide his children how to ward off the coming misfortunes if any.

I

TAKE MUSSOLINI, FOR EXAMPLE!

Did Mussolini, the greatest man of Italy, ever dream that he will die by a hangman's rope? And could he foresee the future of his family and children? Not the least, because he was not interested in Palmistry. He thought man is the master of his own fate and the captain of his own destiny. True, a person is the architect of his own destiny, provided he follows the course that Mother Nature has destined for him and also avoids the pitfalls indicated on the hand.

Mussolini and his family were not interested in Palmistry, and did not provide for the pitfalls. So what sordid fate have they come?

Donna Rachelle Mussolini, now well in her sixties, who became the mother of the Dictator's six children, has been reduced to doing her own washing. She lives in a small, unpretentious villa, and is unable to afford any household assistance. Even during the height of Mussolini's power she was ignored and despised. Now she does everything to avoid the limelight.

Her daughter, Anna Maria, the youngest of the Mussolini children, lived with her until quite recently. Now Anna Maria has gone to join her brother, Vittorio, in Argentina. A victim of infantile paralysis, she is squat, thickset, and mis-shapen.

Romano, her brother, is another weakling. As a youth he suffered from a weak chest, and this condition could not be improved because of a period in a concentration camp after his father's dramatic death. Apart from playing the piano he does nothing.

Vittorio, the best-known of the Dictator's sons after Bruno, who lost his life while testing a bomber, made his escape to Argentina disguised with a beard and dark glasses. There he became a radio producer, and then a commercial traveller. There have been other ventures since then, all equally unsuccessful.

Of all the Mussolini children, the well-known Edda is faring best. After her exile on the penal island of Lopari she is luxuriating on the proceeds of Count Ciano's very successful **Diary** which was smuggled out to her a day or two before her husband was executed.

So this is what fate did to Mussolini's children. And this is what the fate can do to your children, if you ignore the still, silent voice of Palmistry. This science guides you and helps you to provide against all calamities and catastrophies. Nothing is inevitable in the world. All misfortunes can be mended, all evils can be ended. Palmistry is your friend, your near and dear ones' best guide and guru. Why don't you avail of its services? It costs you nothing. It brings you everything.

A pauper can become a prince if only he would get rid of the adverse influences which are pauperizing him and adopt a different course of action. On the contrary, a prince can be pauperized by ignoring the forces which brought him to princedom. Mahatma Gandhi, for example, was the greatest man of India; but which of his sons has risen to the height of his footstool?

II

SECOND WORLD WAR HEROES

Stalin

"Stalin", says Rita Van Alen in You and Your Hand, "is shown to have secretive hands by the very way he unconsciously holds them."

Winston Churchill

Winston Churchill's thumb reveals a personally generous side of his nature. Also his familiar "Thumbs up!" so well known to the world, helped to stiffen the backbone of a very troubled wartorn nation.

American Leaders

Rita Van Alen further believes that General MacArthur has conscientious hands. General Eisenhower has "dependable and conservative hands", Ex-Secretary of State, U.S.A., Mr. Byrnes, has "co-operative hands".

Although Rita Van Alen's prophecy about General Eisenhower was made long before he became the President of U.S.A., his two terms as president amply proved that he was "dependable but conservative". He was so conservative that John Foster Dulles, the lawyer Secretary of State, controlled everything! President Eisenhower obeyed the law of the land in letter and spirit. He kept aloft the torch of American freedom, not knowing whether it was on or off! It was only when the death of Dulles removed the heavy Hand of Law from the head of Eisenhower that he visited India and received one of the greatest receptions in the history of our country.

III

CHEIRO'S PROPHECIES

We do not know what prophecies of Cheiro proved wrong, but we do know a few which proved correct.

Rasputin

With unerring precision, Cheiro predicted the violent death of Rasputin, who was impudent enough to call himself the Saviour of Russia.

While Cheiro was looking at his left hand, he suddenly shouted, "I know my future. You do not know it. My future is to redeem the people and save the Czar from himself".

Cheiro said: "I foresee for you a violent end within a palace. You will be manaced by poison, by knife and by bullet. Finally I see the icy waters of Neva closing above you."

Everybody knows how Rasputin was assassinated. His body was thrown in the icy waters of Neva as predicted by the seer.

Secret of the Mystery of Life

Cheiro predicted the exact hour of his own death. He knew, during his illness, that death was steadily stealing over him. He prepared himself to die.

Before his death, his thoughts flew back to the East, the cradle of his knowledge. He said:

"I KNOW ENOUGH TO REALIZE THAT IN THE EAST LIE THE SECRETS OF THE FUTURE; THE SECRET OF THE MYSTERY OF LIFE—WHY WE ARE HERE AND WHERE WE ARE GOING!"

Chapter Four

THE SIMPLE KEY TO COMPLEX CHARACTER

> The brain. which admittedly houses the mind, is so intimately related with the hand, its most constant servant, that from this point alone, it may be realized that the hand outwardly reflects the personality more revealingly than any other part of the anatomy.
>
> —Rita Van Alen

As a golden key to one's career and character, the deep dive into the mysteries of the mind and the laws of the Lines is not necessary. A fixed and profound peep into the text, the texture and the textile of your hands, or anybody's hands, can bring forth a treasureful of mighty mysteries.

Your hands may be beautiful or ugly, rough or smooth, broad or narrow, well-formed or badly-shaped, short or long, square or oblong, soft or hard, rosy or pale, flabby or stiff, dry or moist, curved or straight, plain or projecting,—all these embody a secret code of character which can be deciphered with a little patience.

I

PHYSIOGNOMY OF PALMISTRY

Captain d' Arpentigny, who fought under Napoleon Bonaparte, is said to have devoted his life and leisure to the general characteristics of the hand as key to the inner impulses of the man.

Gaze cleanly and clearly at the hands to let your heart sip into the head. An approach from hands to the head through the natural occult powers of your heart should be an effortless effort based on natural sympathy.

The impression of the general hand is as important as the expression of its individual lines. The map of the hands should be studied both intensively and extensively to arrive at the correct results.

By simply looking at the hands you can tell whether a person is healthy or sick. Healthy hands reflect a rosy tinge. In unhealthy hands there is a tint of paleness.

As a measure of mental health, rosy hands indicate optimism and pale hands show pessimism.

These were the conclusions of Captain d' Arpentigny some of whose researches saw the light in 1843, and his work is more of scientific than palmistrical nature.

A soft flexible hand indicates adaptability; but when the hand is over-soft and over-flexible, it indicates a nature which can be turned away this side or that by the opinion and will of others, like a flame in the wind or a faxen nose.

A skinny hand, like that of Cassius, shows "hungry look" in a politician or ambitious man, zest for power and suspicion. Too much skinniness shows want of will and energy.

A fleshy hand shows zest and zeal for life and high-living. But too much fleshiness only indicates indolence and shirking of active life.

So you have to watch not only the physical features of the hands, but its different degrees to arrive at right values and not be misled into wrong conclusions altogether.

Importance of Intuition

The importance of intuition cannot be under-rated in the study of the human hand. It is not merely what the hand speaks out on the surface that needs to be studied. Down below from the hand come the radio waves which speak to the Palmist and fingerpoint to the career and character of the subject.

Intuition plays great part in the study of the hand, the head and the heart. Without powers of intuition it would not have been possible for Cheiro to make such prophecies as the death of Lord Kitchner by drowning at sea. Cheiro was not only a palmist but also an occultist. Every great palmist is bound to be that. Hand is only a via media to the head and the heart. By constantly gazing at hands of thousands of people, the via media becomes superfluous and the heart of the subject speaks directly to the heart of the palmist. A mesmeric rapport is established between the two.

"For one interested enough to make extensive research", says Rita Van Alen," there is ample proof to be found that the hand mirrors not only the character of an individual but his aims and ambitions—and even more importantly, his possibilities of achieving them."

II

THE PALMIST AS ARTIST

A palmist must study the hand with as much love and devotion, aesthetic concentration, as an artist studies his model for the purpose of portraiture. The hand must be studied always in all ways to assess the worth and value of the total personality behind it.

"Suppose a great artist were about to make a portrait of you. He would regard the light, the background, would pose you this way or that, to place you at your best advantage and to emphasize your finest features. Then as the painting progressed, more than likely, he would strive to capture something beyond line and colouring, that elusive quality that distinguishes you, more generally known as your personality. . . . Like fragrance flooding a flower, the essence seeps through one, taking expression across the face, the form, the voice, the entire human ensemble, but most especially and expressively through the hands."

Mental Portraiture

Palmistry is the technique of mental portraiture. The mind sees the personality of the subject in a three-dimensional geography. The unconscious and subconscious levels and layers of the mind are mirrored and measured on the coast-to-coast map of the hand. To understand the language of the lines one needs inspection as well as introspection. Those who try to follow the superficial rules and regulations often commit a great error of judgment.

They often mistake the trees for the wood and the wood for the trees. To have clarity at a distance one must have clarity at hand first. To find clarity in the subject's hand, the palmist must have first clarity in his own head.

The signs and symbols on the hand form a staircase down which the palmist descends into the unexplored depths of the subject's soul. Across the threshold of clear-cut conviction he stumbles on the wise wicket of prediction. He can see what is going to happen. He can hear the tread of the future. He can smell the coming events in the breath of the subject. It is through the totality of occult approach that the hand helps us in deciphering the secret code of personality. The hand is only a symbol of symbols. The inner eye sees the hand as the inner and the outer snapshot of the entire personality.

Striking the Balance

After observing the pros and cons, the palmist must strike the balance of the total kaleidoscopic personality of the meanest individuality. Weigh two good points against one bad point to equalize the two, because evil usually goes much further than good, and it is a hundred times more difficult to raise a building than to raze it. Hands speak a lot at first glance; but first impressions are not usually the correct impressions. You must observe the total keyboard before striking the tune of the future.

III

SIZE OF THE HANDS

Large Hands

People with large hands, have a passion for small details. They desire everything to be perfect in its minutest details. They are great sticklers for courtesy, etiquette, formalities and protocol. Smallest thing out of order upsets them. They are conservative by nature and radical changes are not pleasing to them. They make good shopkeepers, priests, lawyers, draughtsmen, commercial artists, copyists, compilers, librarians, housewives, compounders, operation theatre assistants, clerks, routine clerks, file clerks, stenographers, store-keepers, hotel managers, programme secretaries, administrators, drivers, pilots, agents, gardeners, decorators, contractors, commission agents.

Short Hands

People with small hands have a flair for big plans, great schemes. They are generals, conquerors, big business bosses, great dam-builders, prophets, great architects, industrial tycoons, visionaries, creative big-canvas artists, pioneers, leaders of thought and industry blazing new trails of thought and philosophy. They are great daydreamers and visionaries. In their ambitions they are unscrupulous unless backed by other signs. Usually they will stop at nothing in their march to their Golden Goal. Notwithstanding their disregard for high moral principles to attain their ends they fail more often than they succeed. If matched with great moral and mental principles, their chances of success in life are improved. Their very unscrupulousness brings into play a host of indefatigable enemies.

Medium Hand

A medium-sized hand, neither very long nor very short, indicates mental balance and coolness of temper in all eventualities. It is the hand of the lay man who faces all troubles for small family joys. It is the best hand for judges, teachers, arbitrators, inspectors, accountants, treasurers, railway guards, watch and ward department. Most of the common people have indeed medium hands and they form the very backbone of democracy.

Hollow Hand

A hollow hand indicates an empty pocket and a financial failure. People with hollow hands have hollow fortunes. Time and tide are against them. They struggle

against heavy odds. Success is not impossible for them
but it is certainly very difficult. People with hollow hands
are like Gaetano Pisani in **Zanoni:**—

> Gaetano Pisani's talents as a composer had been
> chiefly exhibited in music appropriate to this his fav-
> ourite instrument, of all unquestionably the   most
> various and royal in its resources and power over
> the passions. As Shakespeare among poets, is the
> cremona among the instruments.   Nevertheless, he
> had composed other pieces, of larger ambition and
> larger accomplishment, and, chief of these his pre-
> cious—his unpurchased—his unpublished—his unpub-
> lishable and imperishable, opera of the "Siren". This
> great work had been the dream of his boyhood—the
> mistress of his manhood; in advancing age "it stood
> beside him like his youth". Vainly had he struggled
> to place it before the world. Even bland unjealous
> Paisiello, Maestro di Capella, shook his gentle head
> when the musician favoured him with specimen of
> one of his most thrilling scenes. And yet, Paisiello,
> though that music differs from all Durante taught
> thee to emulate—but patience, Gaetano Pisani!—
> bide thy tune, and keep thy violin in tune!

Swollen Hand

A swollen hand indicates lethargy, liver trouble, lack
of energy, love of ease and pleasure, contempt for hard
work, cruelty of nature, indifference to moral principles,
lip service to religion, conservative nature, let-the-sleep-
ing-dogs-lie mentality, escapism, fatality, callousness, inability to mix with the masses, inability to forget injury,
false pride, and ironical kind of humour. This is the
hand of the drunken sensual person. Such people live
fast and die early. They are moody temperamental people. They can do anything. But usually they do nothing. They have a will but no sustaining power behind it.

IV

TEXTURE OF HANDS

Soft Hand

People with soft hands have lovable artistic nature. They are of poetical and musical mind. They are poets by nature even if they write no poetry. They are ruled by imagination rather than the intellect. It is essentially a feminine hand. Even in a masculine hand it shows feminine nature, the milk of human kindness. Men with such hands have more of woman in their nature. They compassionate and sympathetic.

Flabby Hands

People with flabby hands are lazy, lethargic, apathetic, callous, indifferent, sensual, ease-loving, selfish and completely heartless. They think the world exists for them but they do not exist for the world. They are deceiving by habit and treacherous by nature. For them morality is only an instrument to hoodwink others. They preach high morality to others but never think of practising it themselves. I think parliaments of the world today abound with flabby hands, people who gatecrash anywhere through sheer financial powers.

Hard Hand

The hard hand belongs to an industrious man. It is the hand of the practical worker, whether he handles a machine or the minds of men. It indicates a straightforward disposition. He is steadfast and reliable. He can bear hardship without murmur. It is the hand of the mechanical worker. When Lenin said, "Workers of the world, unite!" he was thinking of the people with hard hands, not the politicians with flabby hands who make workers their political instruments.

Heavy Hand

It is the hand of the cruel man who oppresses others just for the show of his authority and ego. It is the hand of a sadist who finds joy in cruelty. It is the professional hand of a hangsman, executioner, traitor and blackmarketeer.

Thin Hand

A thin hand shows want of zest and zeal, sickness and lack of energy. It also indicates femininity to a fault and a desire to be treated tenderly like a lily. It also shows meanness of mind and poverty of intellect.

Thick Hand

Thick hand shows grossness of instincts, sensuality, callousness, unprincipled life, want of wider vision, narrowmindedness, selfishness, distrust in others, whimsicality, superstition, mental fearfulness matched with a public bravado, obstinacy without stamina.

V

COLOUR OF HANDS

Pink Hand

Pinkness of hand is a sign of health, highmindness and optimism of outlook. It shows mutual love, common sympathy, universal compassion. It is the hand of one who can feel for himself and others. He has a genial and gentle spirit. He has an abounding enthusiasm. He is confident and trustworthy. He can trust others and others can trust him.

Red Hand

Pink is good but red is bad. Red hands, indicate intensity of passions, quickness of temper, drunkenness, and cruelty.

"The red palm is the sign of the hard driver. To such a one laziness is a cardinal crime. Anything can be forgivenness but this. It is the hand of activity and impatience."

White Hand

A white hand is a symbol of milk-white beauty, extreme delicacy, or just colourlessness.

Dead-White Hand

A dead-white hand shows coldness, want of enthusiasm, lack of ardour, hospitality, heat and warmth. It is a sign of vanity, cold emotions, extreme sophistication, or just approaching death.

Black Hands

Black hands show dyspepsia, colic temperament, inefficient lungs, heart trouble, liver disorder, guilty conscience, profound sorrow.

WEATHER OF HANDS

Wet Hands

A hand perpetually moist is an indication of hard work, industriousness, anxiety, desire to show forth one's best in the world, go-ahead spirit despite all obstacles, enthusiasm and warm-bloodedness, optimism. It shows vivacity of spirit and warmth of emotions. It is a proof of great physical activity.

Perspiring Hand

A habitually perspiring hand shows a phlegmatic temperament. It also shows sensuality and love of ease, luxury and idleness.

Dry Hands

Dry hands show practicality and evenness of temper and a balance unemotional outlook on life.

Cold Hands

Either the person is physically weak and lacks proper food and energy or he is cold and calculating, a man of suspicious nature like Emperor Aurangzabe. A man with cold hands cannot trust anybody. The man is reserved and unemotional.

Warm Hands

Warm hands show vivacity of spirit, hasty temperament. and personal magnetism.

Hot Hands

Hot hands are an indication of high temperature and fever, needing immediate medical attention. If a friend is trying to conceal his illness from you, a handshake will tell the truth.

VII

MISCELLANEOUS

Rough Hands

Rough hands, if these are not due to the nature of profession in which one is engaged, show deceptive mind and inartistic nature. Such people talk a lot, but all their talk is to hide the true nature of their designs against you—deception. You have to be on your guard.

Extra-Smooth Hands

Extra-smooth hands in person other than a woman should be treated with a pinch of salt. Such a person shirks work, wastes his time in self-adornment and lives through confidence trickery.

Misshapen Hands

Misshapen hands do not always indicate a misshapen mind, if the other indications are good. The man may be a critic, cynic or a philosopher. Misshapen hands may be due to old age. But in a perfectly normal man these are proof of extreme perversities and you must tread carefully in the company of such a person.

VIII

FACT-FINDING FACTORS

While examining the text, texture, textile, colour, atmosphere, etc. of the hands, as mentioned above, take care of the following factors in each individual case:—

i. Sex
ii. Age
iii. Profession
iv. Mood and emotion
v. Size of the body
vi. General health
vii. Weather conditions
viii. Heritage
ix. Economic conditions
x. Family atmosphere.

Chapter Five

THE CARICATURE OF YOUR CAREER

We ought to define the hand as belonging exclusively to man, corresponding in its sensibility and emotion, to the endowment of the mind.

—Sir Charles Bell

Every human hands holds a convex and concave mirror to the character and career of a man whose entire future is there, although slightly distorted, and it does not require a great palmist to decipher it. You know your career. And you know your hand. Just see your hand carefully and you will see how it is a faithful portrait of your professional activities. For instance, you will find that the hand of a mechanic will be rough and tough, while that of a writer will generally be soft and smooth. One who holds the pen will have a far better shape for his hand than one who strikes a hammer on the anvil in a red-hot smithy.

Even though Carlyle was a "bull who learnt to handle a pen" (as Walt Whitman called him!), his hands must be vastly different from a bullman or a bull-fighter, not to speak of a bull. One writing pastoral poetry must have vastly different hands than one not yet out of a pastoral civilization.

The simple shape of a hand can tell a lot about the career and character of a man. Long before you come to study of the palm, you can have a general impression about the behaviour and behaviourism of a gentleman or a lady. In fact, a man may be unwilling to show you your hand, but he cannot conceal the general shape unless he keeps his hands neatly and nicely tucked in his pant pockets, perpetually which is an impossibility unless a person is an imbecile.

The varying shapes of hands determine the suitability or otherwise of a person for the profession he is following or intends to take up or whether he should adopt it or not. Just from a general distant survey of a stranger's hand you can tell whether he is an artist, which he is supposed to be, or just an artisan.

It is said about Henry Ford that he could tell from the sound of a machine as to which country it belonged. When a friend wanted to test Benjamin Franklin, who was a wool expert, by showing him a sample of wool in England, after blindfolding him, Franklin told him: "It is not wool at all, only dog's hair!"

If blindfolded Franklin could distinguish between wool and dog's hair, unblindfolded you can certainly tell from his shape of hands whether a man is a poet, politician, prophet, priest, philosopher, pensioner, prospector, or just pickpocket!

I

THE ELEMENTARY HAND

The elementary hand is a hand without a proper figure. Coarse and clumsy, it belongs to the lowest level of human development. It has short fingers. Its palm is thick and heavy. This human hand closely resembles that of a monkey. The fingers are shorter than the palm as in animals. According to Dr. Cairn, "The bones of the palm form, among the brutes, almost the whole palm."

An elementary hand has more of the palm than the fingers. While the fingers are short and clumsy, the palm is thick and coarse.

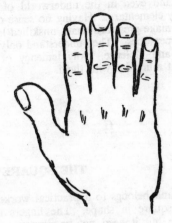

Elementary Hand

These are the characteristics of people with elementary hands:—

    i. Little mental development.

    ii. No intellectual understanding.

    iiii. No sense of culture and civilization.

    iv. No finer feelings of friendship or love.

    v. No love but only lust.

    vi. No control over passions and desires.

    vii. No regard for public morals.

    viii. No love of beauty or art.

    ix. No appreciation of music.

    x. No reason, but only instinct.

You can still find these people in the tribal areas of India, the forests of Africa and the backwoods of

America. They are more akin to animals than to men.
People with perfect Elementary Hands you do not find
in the cities. But there are plenty of people in rustic
areas of India and even in the underworld of Chicago
who are partially elementary. Having no sense of morality, such people make great criminals, unskilled labourers,
soldiers, and desperadoes. They understand only the language of force and violence. Any leniency or persuasion does not cut much ice with them.

II

THE SQUARE HAND

The Square Hand belongs to a practical worker. The
palm is almost square in shape. The fingers are also
sometimes square but it need not be always so. The
palm can also be square at the wrist. Sometimes even
the nails are square. When everything is square, the man
is a pure square type But such perfection is rare. Usually only the palm is square.

People with Square Hands are devoted to duty and
discipline. They are active workers. Hamlet's philosophical "To Be Or Not To Be" has no appeal for them.
They serve, they suffer, without a prick of conscience.
They take both joy and sorrow in the stride. Everyday
is a new day for them. They waste no time in idle brood-
ing.

They are practical, precise and punctual. They love
discipline and respect authority. They are on the whole
a law-abiding people who are more interested in bringing
up a family than bringing out a revolution. They have
no mind and moment to think of others. They are too

much full of their own day-to-day engagements. They love work. Idleness tires them.

They are conservative by nature and slaves to custom by habit. They are argumentative, ready to fight for what they regard as their rights. Public welfare is not their concern. They are interested in what the people can do for them, not what they can do for the people.

They waste no time in poetry and arts. Money-making is their main occupation. They want to keep up social appearances but are not interested in social success as an ideal of life. They are ready to suffer in the present for a future advantage.

They love home and family. They perform domestic duties as holy writ. They have a force of character and will-power which can become stubbornness if resisted.

The Punjab peasants who make good farmers, good traders, good mechanics, taxi-drivers, truck-drivers, and are successful not only all over India but also in U.K., Canada and U.S.A. are people with square hands.

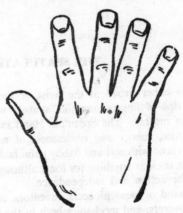

Square Hand

Variations of Character

Square hand with short square fingers—a narrow materialistic type who cannot think beyond personal gain.

Square hand with long square fingers: people with sense and sensibility beyond moneymaking.

Square hand with knotty fingers: love of detail and philosophical bent of mind.

Square hand with spatulate fingers: great mechanical powers. "Finest useful mechanism has been turned out by men with the square hands and spatulate fingers."

Square hand with conic fingers: makes a good commercial artist or poet. His art is not high but pays.

Square hand with mixed fingers: great versatility of ideas.

III

THE SPATULATE HAND

The palm is either broad at the wrist or the base of fingers. The tips of fingers resemble spatula which the chemists use in mortar. The Spatulate Hand indicates a love of adventure, energy and restlessness of nature.

A Spatulate Hand with soft and flabby palm lacks stickativeness, cannot stick at anything for long, although he has a great love for action and independence.

This is the hand of great pioneers, inventors, engineers, explorers, discoverers, and mechanics both in the world of matter and mind, both the theoretical and practical side

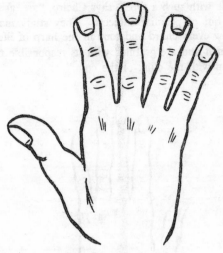

Spatulate Hand

where expansion is desirable. The actors, teachers, politicians and professionals with such hands blaze new trails of ideas and ideals.

IV

THE ANGULAR HAND

The Angular Hand is long with bony fingers. It has rather long nails and well-developed joints. This is the hand of the philosophers for whom wisdom is superior to weal or wealth.

"People with such a type", says Cheiro, "are, as a rule, students but of peculiar subjects. They study mankind, they know every chord and tone in the harp of life; they play upon it and are gratified with its responsible melody more than with the clink of the coin."

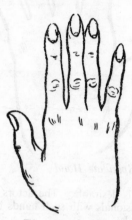

The Angular Hand

Such people have idealistic ambitions in which money plays a subsidiary role. They love the mysterious, the hidden and the unknown. They make good mind-readers, psychopaths, telepathists, occultists, hypnotists, psychiatrists. They are profound thinkers, silent and secretive by habit and nature. They make excellent thinkers, philosophers, mystics, Yogis, saints, reformers, prophets, oracles, teachers and preachers.

V

THE CONIC HAND

The conic hand has a tapering palm. The fingers are conic or slightly pointed. The tip of the nail phalanx is pointed too. Persons with conic hands are inspirational, instinctive and impulsive. They have a love of ease and luxury. They are quick to theorize but slow to practise. They make very good plans but these are all visionary. They are good conversationalists and at home with people who do not know them intimately and so can be easily taken in. They create a very good first impression, but they are changeable in affection. They are extreme in their likes and dislikes. They are sentimental and temperamental moody men and women. They are influenced by colour, music, joy, love and romance of life. They

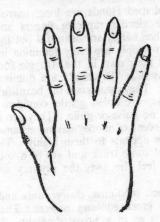

The Conic Hand

cannot sustain their interests in any occupation for long. Change is the need of their nature. They make good leaders of revolution but seldom reap the harvest of rewards.

When the conic hand is hard, it is a welcome sign, because it shows firmness of will added to creative philosophical nature. People with Conic Hands make good leaders of public life but make no material profits for themselves. They are led away by their emotions and can be easily tipped over when not wanted.

VI

ALMOND-SHAPED HAND

The Almond-shaped Hands are long, narrow and fragile. They have slender tapering fingers and almond-shaped nails. Thee hands are beautiful but indicate lack of energy. Such people are truly feminine in character and cannot hold their own in the struggle for existence. Such people known as "Psychics", are dominated by an idealistic nature. They appreciate the beautiful but make poor artists. They are quiet, gentle, confident and trustworthy, knowing no guise or guile. They are ignorant of business and innocent of moneymaking schemes. Music, colour and dance appeals to them highly. They are always in search of some truth and are of a spiritual bent of mind. They feel the awe, the mystery and majesty of life.

They make good mediums, clairvoyants and spiritualists. They have great guessing powers. They can see the coming events as in a broad daylight. They make good occultists. They tend to become morose and morbid and melancholy. If not properly nursed and nurtured, they end in lunatic asylums.

Cheiro described these people in a picturesque language:—

> "They are lilies thrown, by some ruthless hand, upon the tempest-tossed river of life . . . they seem so helpless in the forward sweep of that terrible current. One sees them at times clinging to banks for pity. Ah! these beautiful hands have no strength; they are swept on again by the rising tide of bubbling, frothy humanity."

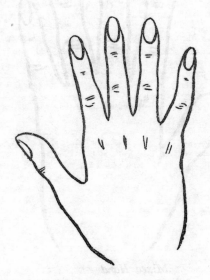

The Almond-shaped Hand

VII

THE MIXED HAND

The Mixed Hand has no particular shape.   It combines qualities and characteristics of all the hands mentioned above.   It cannot be classed or classified.   The palm may

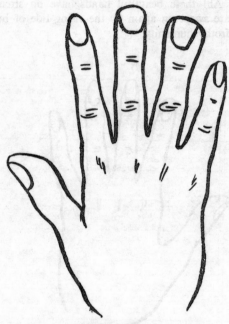

Mixed Hand

be square, spatulate, conic, angular or almond-shaped.
Five fingers may belong to different categories.

The Mixed Hand is the mixture of all human qualities,
good as well as bad. It is a symbol of versatility. It
shows a vastness of ideas matched with a changeability
of purpose. The Mixed Hand can easily adapt itself to
the circumstances and adapt the circumstances to itself.
He can play to the gallery and win laurels without becoming a martyr to theories. He borrows freely and
makes it his own. William Shakespeare must be having
a Mixed Hand.

Emerson writes in **Letters and Social Aims,** "When
Shakespeare is charged with debt to his authors, Landor
replies, 'Yet he was more original than his originals. He
breathed upon dead bodies and brought them into life."

That is the quality of a Mixed Hand. He can improve
upon what he borrows from others. Such persons have
tact, technique, trade-tricks and make magnificent dip-
lomats and go-betweens. They are fond of action and
adventure.

Chapter Six

POSING A CAREER?

Why should not the hand give the characteristics of man's physiognomy, since the hand is the medium of manifestation of human action

—Balzac

Are you trying to pose a career? You cannot pose a career when you pose your hands. The position of your hands reveals your character and your career. Your hand-position speaks out your head-position.

I

PSYCHOLOGY OF HANDS

The psychology of the position of hands has been very well studied by William G Benham in **The Laws of Scientific Hand Reading**, who lays down this dictum:—

"It may be stated here that the hand whose owner has little or nothing to hide opens itself freely to the gaze, and that the hand of one whose deeds and thoughts will not bear the inspection wishes to hide itself, or to close the fingers over the palm, studiously concealing it from sight. The mind feels the necessity of hiding its workings and the fingers obeying the suggestion, close over the palm."

Thus all actions of man are betrayed by the manner in which he poses his hands. By his unconscious action he may reveal exactly what he is trying to conceal and cover up.

II

SIGNS AND SYMBOLS

Hands Clasped Behind the Back

This is a very frequent pose. Such a person is extremely cautious. He does not want to harm anybody. Only he is trying to protect himself from the harm of others. He is an accountant, a partner in a firm, a man with many rivals, planner facing practical difficulties, a person who should like to trust others but finds people untrustworthy.

Heavy Limping Hands Like that of a Corpse

The man is probably a mechanic returning home dead tired. He is a dense and coarse person. If he poses to be a gentleman or scholar, he cannot be so. He is too much physically tired for any sort of intellectual activity.

Palm Upwards Fingers held Loosely

The person is full of self-importance. He imagines he will top I.A.S. competition, but there is no work behind his supposition. He should roll up his sleeves and better get to work soon.

Tightly-Clenched Fist

This is typical of the bully. Beware of him if he says "Hey, Mister!" He cannot be your friend. He can only be your master. He is looking for a slave, not even a servant.

Rubbing Hands Together

You cannot depend upon such a person. He is a slippery fellow, washing his hands of all previous sins and crimes. He is getting ready for new hypocritical and untruthful conquests. If he says he will help you, he is only planning to harm you. He might well be a cutthroat or confidence trickster or gambler or spy or backbiter who exploits your difficulties.

Heavy Limping Hands

Palm on Palm

When palm is resting on palm, the man might well be a yogi, a Sri Krishna, a person of even temper who is ready to be of use to others by way of advice if not assistance. You can trust him. He can be a good secretary, adviser or counsellor.

Waving Hands

A person with waving hands is of suspicious nature. He will never believe you even if you tell him the whole truth. He expects everybody to tell a lie. He is grandiloquent man whose tongue is an instrument of his trade. He might well be a salesman trying to sell a cat in the bag.

Palm on Palm

Toying Hands

A person toying with buttons, handkerchief, etc. is under a temporary nervous excitement. His mind is out of joint. Do not take him on his word. He might use you as a cat's paw to pull his chestnuts out of the fire—and then forget you. Do not run any risk for him however honeyed may be his persuasion.

Right Forearm Vertical

If the right forearm is vertical and the fingers are closed gracefully, it indicates a nature dominated by artistic qualities. This is the characteristic pose of a trustworthy woman. You can trust her, however low she might be stationed.

Right Hand Drooping

If the right hand is drooping and the left hand is swaying, it betrays an extremely fanicky nature. The man is hypersensitive and shows an excess of feminity.

Hands that Find No Place

There are persons who seem to find no place for their hands. Sometimes they carry their hands up, sometimes down, sometimes in pockets, sometimes on wrist watches, etc. Such people are uncertain of their purpose. They have a strong character, but their mind is indecisive. They should make up their minds fully, firmly and finally before launching on a career. As your employees, they will leave you in the lurch at any time. Don't employ such people. If they are already in your employment, dismiss them.

Hands that find no Place

Hiding Hands

Hiding of hands from the view of others indicates a shady side of character. The person is deceitful, untruthful and hypocritical. If you believe the reverse of what he says, you may be nearer the truth. He may be a property dealer, contractors, spurious salesman, backbiter, or confidence trickster. He can be a criminal, ex-convict, cheat or murderer.

Hiding Hands

Fingers Partially Closed

When fingers are only partially closed, the person is cautious but not untrustworthy. He is trying to guard himself but has no intention of harming others. He might well be a banker, pawn-broker, financier, secret service man, spy.

Limping Dangling Hands

Most of the students in schools and colleges have limp and dangling hands. It indicates indecision and lack of fixed purpose. Such person cannot keep secrets. They are yet to be initiated into the hard school of life. They have not yet found their feet.

Hanging Hands Closed Fists

This is the indication of one who is labouring under a great determination. It might well show a student making up his mind about taking a competitive examination. The clenched fist shows that the person is ready for the battle. It shows the shunting in of vital energy.

Fingers Partially Closed

Chapter Seven

FATE'S FIVE-FINGERED FUTURITY

It is a remarkable fact that we cannot feel the pulse with the tongue, but we can with the fingers.

—Sir Charles Bell

Fingers sum up the entire Hindu philosophy of fate, fatalism, fatality and futurity, extending from birth to birth. The Hindu saying "Five fingers are not equal" is the greatest philosophical counterblast to the Communist thesis of socialistic equalisation. Mentally, morally and materially, equality is against the laws of nature. I know a friend who is a Chief Officer while his brother is a peon in the same establishment of the Government of India, both equal sons of the same father but not equal children of the same fate.

"I comprehend you", said Glydon, "you will not allow the law of universal equality".

"Law!" said Zanoni, "If the world conspired to enforce the falsehood, they could not make it a law. Level all conditions today, and you only smooth away all obstacles to tyranny tomorrow. A nation that aspires to **equality** is unfit for **freedom.** Throughout all creation, from the archangel to the worm, from Olympus to the pebble, from the radiant and completed planet to the nebula that hardens through ages of mist and slime into the habitable world, the first law of nature is inequality."

"Harsh doctrine, if applied to states. Are the cruel disparities of life never to be removed?"

"Disparities of the physical life? Oh, let us hope so. But disparities of the **intellectual** and the **moral**, never! Universal equality of intelligence, of mind, of genius, of virtue!—no teacher left the world, no man wiser, better than others—were it not an impossible condition, **what a hopeless prospect for humanity!** No; while the earth lasts, the sun will gild the mountain top before it shines upon the plain."

I

FINE FINGER PHILOSOPHY

The philosophy of the fingers has interested not only the Palmists but also the Scientists. Sir Isaac Newton said, "Lacking necessary proofs, a study of the fingers, and particularly the thumb of man, would convince me of the existence of God." Sir Charles Bell has made a more exhaustive study of the physiological mysteries that lie embedded in the fingers of a man:—

"The cuticle is so far a part of the organ of touch that it is the medium through which the external impression is conveyed to the nerves. The extremities of the fingers best exhibit the provisions for the exercise of this sense. The nails give support to the tips of the fingers and in order to sustain the elastic cushion that forms their extremities they are made broad and shieldlike. This cushion is an important part of the exterior apparatus. Its fullness and elasticity adapt it admirably for the touch. It is a remarkable fact that we cannot feel the palse with the tongue, but that we can with the fingers. On a nearer inspection we discover in the points of fingers a more particular provision for adapting them to touch. Whenever the sense of feeling is more exquisite, there we see minute spiral ridges of the cuticle. These ridges have corresponding depressions on the inner surface, and they again give lodgement to soft pulpy processes of the skin called papillae, in which lie the extremities of the sentiment nerves. Thus the nerves are adequately protected, while they are at the same time sufficiently exposed to have impressions communicated to them through the elastic cuticle and thus give rise to the sense of touch."

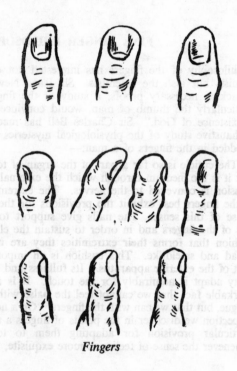

Fingers

II

FIVE STARRY FINGERS

Five Fingers, which are named after the stars, are pilot planets in the firmaments of your destiny. They are named as follows:—

1. **Jupiter Finger** The first finger, also known as the Index Finger.
2. **Saturn Finger** This is the second finger.
3. **Apollo Finger** This is the third finger.
4. **Mercury Finger** This is the fourth finger, also known as the little finger.

The thumb will be dealt with separately in the next chapter.

III

LENGTH OF FINGERS

The length of fingers can only be judged in proportion to the body as a whole. Length and shortness are relative terms.

Long Fingers

Long-fingered people are minute-minded men and women. They are interested in small details of the activities entrusted to them or those which they entrust to others. They are also of whimsical and suspicious character. They want everybody to depend on them but they

cannot depend on anybody. As politicians they want
to conduct the government as a small department store.

"Emperor Aurangzabe, well-known for his political sus-
picions and the consequent downfall of the Moghal Em-
pire, had long fingers. Like all long-fingered people,
Aurangzeb was sensitive, methodical and possessed a good
memory. He was also unsympathetic and cold-blooded.
He was not fond of granting favours. Nevertheless, there
was something refined in his nature, and he seemed learned."

The long-fingered people do not allow the small affairs
to pass unnoticed. But they lack the broad vision and
consideration of bigger issues which they cannot see in
a proper perspective. Verily, they can see a straw in the
eyes of others but not a beam in their own.

Short Fingers

The short-fingered people concentrate on the bigger issues of life. Petty details do not fascinate them. Napoleon Bonaparte was probably a man with short fingers.
The short-fingered people see the events telescopically and
act quickly without mincing matters. The question of
details does not bother them. They think briskly and
jump to the conclusions. They are fond of pomp and
show, impulse and hot-headed children of nature. They
are fond of big things. As engineers they love to design
big buildings, dams and splendid projects. They cannot
make small artistic huts. As generals they lead armies.
As businessmen they control kartels and corporations,
combines and monopolies. In the panorama of big planning they leave the details to be filled in by their assistants.

Medium Hands

People with medium hands are middle-of-the-road workers. They are conservative and shun extremes. Radical

views do not appeal to them. They are common workers, most practical people, "divine averages" (Walt Whitman's phrase), and down-t-earth thinkers.

IV

LITTLE LAWS OF LENGTH

Jupiter Finger

i. Long—love of authority, command and dictatorial nature.
ii. Very long—extreme self-conceit and despotic nature.
iii. Short—dislike for responsibility.
iv. Very short—timidity and non-aggressiveness.
v. Crooked—lack of political aspiration.

Saturn Finger

i. Long—caution.
ii. Very long—morbid suspicion.
iii. Short—lack of practical intelligence.
iv. Very short—silliness.
v. Crooked—hysteria.

Apollo Finger

Long—devotion to the beautiful.
Very long—morbid aestheticism, art-criticism.
Short—no love for fame.
Very short—love for obscurity.
Crooked—fear of publicity.

Mercury Finger

Long—great commercial qualities.
Very long—desire for blackmarketing and business malpractices.
Short—confusion of mind in business affairs.
Crooked—business jealousy.

V

PARTS OF FINGERS

Phalanges

The sections of fingers are called phalanges. Each finger has three phalanges.

First Phalanx—between the tip and the nearest joint.
Second Phalanx—the middle section.
Third Phalanx—portion joining the palm.

i. If the first phalanx is the longest—predominance of mental powers.
ii. If the second phalanx is the longest—business acumen.
iii. If the third phalanx is the longest—love for eating and drinking; an appreciation of good cookery; taste for hotel and catering business.
iv. If three phalanges are equal—well-balanced life, moral, mental and monetary, equilibrium of Mind, Body and Soul.
v. If the third phalanx is long, narrow and waistlike —love for money and material aggrandizement.
vi. If the fingers are very long with very wide chinks— desire for peeping through the keyhole; spying on others; great detective aptitude.

The Tips of Fingers

    i. Fingers with Square Tips—proof of an orderly mind. Love for method, system, discipline, and regularity. Contempt for disorder and untidiness.

    ii. Fingers with Spatulate Tips: Strong commonsense; fondness for action, sports, games and races.

    iii. Fingers with Pointed Tips—unpractical person; one who builds an ivory tower in a rose garden.

    iv. Fingers with Conic Tips—an artistic nature, impulse and impressionable; love for beauty, art and music.

VI

ANGLES OF FINGERS

On a Slightly Curved Line

If the fingers are set on a slightly curved line, across the palm at the base of fingers—indication of easy success in life and smooth-sailing.

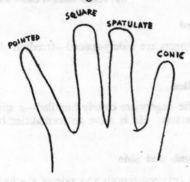

The Tips of Fingers

Set Low

If the fingers are set low, as if pushed into the palm—the subject will lose much of his power and authority.

Finger of Jupiter Low

If the finger of Jupiter is set low—awkwardness in so-social life, like that of the professor in the picture **Blue Angel.**

Finger of Apollo Low

If the finger of Apollo is set low—want of desire for distinction in life.

VII

SPACES BETWEEN FINGERS

Widely Spaced

When the fingers are widely-spaced—freedom of thought and action.

Closely Bundled

When all the fingers are closely bundled—a stiff, stingy and selfish person. He is slave to formalities but lacks sincerity.

Between Thumb and Side

Wide space between thumb and side of the hand—love of freedom and generosity.

Between Saturn and Apollo

Wide space between the fingers of Saturn and Apollo —disregard for future consequences of present actions.

Between Jupiter and Saturn

Wide space between the fingers of Jupiter and Saturn —disregard for formalities and conventions.

Between Apollo and Mercury

Wide space between the fingers of Apollo and Mercury —disregard for the opinions of others; courage of conviction and independence of mind. The person does not care a fig for the ideas of others. He follows his own road. He carves his own niche.

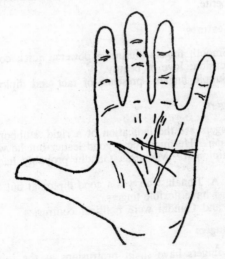

Spaces between Fingers

VIII

FIVE-FINGERED STARS

Finger Cushions

i. Want of finger cushions on the inside of finger-tips—lack of tact and diplomacy.

ii. Over-developed finger cushions—over-sensitiveness, even morbidity.

Finger Size

i. Slightly spare, flattened fingers—ascetic qualities.

ii. Thick fingers—love of comfort and material appetite.

Finger Textures

i. Smooth fingers—intuitive powers; quick comprehension; love of beauty.

ii. Supple fingers—presence of tact and diplomacy.

Stiff Fingers

Stiff fingers are the indication of a rigid, stubborn, inflexible man. He might be a good leader but he will be a poor diplomat. Mahatma Gandhi probably had stiff fingers.

Mr. M. A. Jinnah, who was a good diplomat but a bad leader must have flexible fingers.

Jinnah and Gandhi were political contraries.

Knotty Fingers

Knotty fingers have slight protrusions at the joints if not caused by rheumatism or other diseases.

People with knotty fingers are good critics, logicians, argumentators, lawyers, debaters, parliamentarians, orators, analysers, scientific thinkers.

Knotty fingers indicate the capacity to grasp the situation properly and quickly. People with knotty fingers are best for scientific research work.

Chapter Eight

KNOT YOUR CAREERS!

For the accomplishment of whatever is great and lofty, the clear perception of truths is the first requisite—truths adopted to the object desired.

The warrior thus reduces the chances of battle to combinations almost of mathematics. He can predict a result, if he can but depend upon the materials he is forced to employ. At such a loss he can cross the bridge; in such a time, he can reduce the fort. Still more accurately, for he depends less on material causes than ideas at his command, can the commander of the purer science or divine art, if he once perceives the truths that are in him and around, foretell what he can achieve, and in what he is condemned to fail.

But this perception of truths is disturbed by many causes—vanity, passion, fear, indolence in himself, ignorance of the fitting means without to accomplish what he designs. He may miscalculate his forces; he may have no chart of the country he would invade. It is only in a peculiar state of the mind that it is capable of perceiving truth; and that state is profound serenity.

—Bulwer Lytton

The Knotted Fingers are the fingers of philosophy, the fingers of serenity, the fingers of practical wisdom, the fingers of spiritual clarity, the fingers of a saint and a sage, a Confucius or a Buddha, a Plato, an Aristotle, or a great military strategist like Mao Tse-tung who has converted the Himalayan Indian Wall into the Chinese Highway for the conquest of India.

The joints between the phalanges of fingers bulge visibly in knotted fingers, while in smooth fingers no knots can be seen or felt.

I

KNOTTY OR SMOOTHY?

There are some clear-cut differences of character in people with knotted fingers and those with smooth fingers.

Knotted Fingers	Smooth Fingers
i. Thinking	Action
ii. Thought without action	Action without thought
iii. Political Science	Politics
iv. Poet or philosopher	Journalist or story-writer
v. Guided by reason	Guided by intuition
vi. Governed by the head	Governed by the heart
vii. Classical in life	Romantic in life
viii. Guided by facts	Driven by fancy
ix. Sails in the sea of life guided by the beacon	Stumbles blindly in the wood of life
x. Works under dominant ideas	Works under dominant impulse
xi. Helped by second thoughts	Betrayed by second thoughts
xii. Needs promptitude	Needs stickativeness
xiii. Second thoughts are best	First thoughts are best
xiv. A clear thinker	A clear worker

xv. A confused worker   A confused thinker
xvi. Needs good assist-   Needs good advisers
     ants

II

KNOTTED CAREERS

Fingers with First Joint Knotted

This is a typical philosopher's hand, like that of Confucius or Plato. It indicates great analytical powers and profound insight and an overwhelming intellectual capacity.

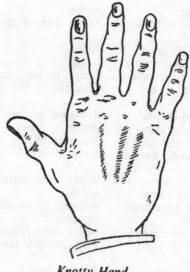

Knotty Hand

Fingers with Second Joint Knotted

Fingers with second joint knotted are indicators of great love for material things. He has a fondness for maintaining discipline and order in everyday affairs of life. Any kind of disorder or untidiness upsets him. He loves classification, system and arrangements. This is the hand of the research scholar, scientific worker, and manager of a great department store.

Fingers With Both Joints Knotted

People with both joints knotted are ruled by fair play and impartiality. They are good judges. They are also people with strong commonsense. They make good engineers, scientists and mathematicians.

Fingers having Bulging Knots on Both Joints

This is an exaggeration of critical qualities. Such people lack imagination and harbour a contempt for the beautiful things of life. They are music-haters and fanatics. They lack interest in poetry and art. They have a low standard in ideals of thought and action.

III

MEANING OF KNOTS

The knots of Fingers are the Knots of Fate. They have great careers and promises entangled in them, but these have to be carefully unravelled. These are knots of great psychological problems.

The knots must be carefully observed while examining the hands. They may form the very key to the character of the person concerned. These should be observed very carefully. These should be interpreted very cautiously, because even a mechanic may have both the joints knotted without becoming a philosopher. His knots are due to the professional strain and stress.

Knots may also be due to some accident or physical deformity, having nothing to do with the signs of palmistry. Allowance must be made for determining their value.

Let us continue Bulwer Lytton's quotation with which we opened the chapter:—

> Your mind is fevered by a desire for truth: you would compel it to your embraces; you would ask me to impart to you, without ordeal or preparation, the grandest secrets that exist in nature. But truth can no more be seen by the mind unprepared for it, than the sun can dawn upon the mdst of might. Such a mind receives truth only to pollute it; to use the simile of one who has wandered near the secret of the sublime Goetia (or the magic that lies within nature, as electricity within the cloud), 'He who pours water into the muddy well, does but disturb the mud'.
> **(Lamb de Vit. Pythag)**

Chapter Nine

A SYMBOL OF AUTHORITY

The thumb is a symbol of authority, of power. In every age, the thumb has played a conspicuous part in the world. In India the thumb is the centre and foundation of the Hindu Palmistry.

—Cheiro

The Thumb goes **thump, thump, thump** in the Corridors of Time. It has been the heavy symbol of authority, of command, of conquest, of despotism and dictatorship down the sweep of the centuries. A person with a weak thumb has never been a ruler, not even in a degenerate democracy.

As Aristotle said, "The superiority of man over animals is in the hand. His superiority over other men is in the thumb." As D. Arpentigny said, "Thumb individualizes the man." The thumb is also the entire man in a miniature. It is a tiny replica of the total personality.

I

INDEX TO DISEASE

A thumb is a great indicator of internal troubles. Cheiro has elaborated this point:—

"The most significant of all is that which relates to what is known in medical work as the 'thumb centre' of the brain. It is a well-known fact among the specialists of nervous diseases that by the examination of the thumb they can tell if the patient is affected or is likely to be affected by paralysis or not, as thumb will indicate such a likelihood a long time before there has appeared the slightest trace of such a disease in any part of the system. If it indicates such an affection, an operation is at once performed on the thumb centre of the brain, and if that operation is successful (which is again shown by the thumb) they have baffled the disease and the patient saved."

Palmistry is yet in its infancy, and Thumb Palmistry is quite raw and green. In not very distant future we

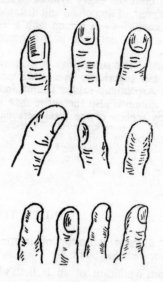

Different kinds of Thumbs

may have Medical Palmistry which is far more sure of its indications than any superficial diagnosis.

II

LENGTH OF THUMB

Long Thumb

The person will use his intellectual powers and practical intelligence to outwit his enemies.

Short and Thick

The subject will employ violence at an opportune moment successfully for the achievement of his ends.

Medium-Sized

When the thumb is medium-sized, the subject will work with dignity and use violence only in the last resort.

Small Thumb

Indicates timidity, weakness of will and purpose. Gandhiji warned small-thumbed people when he said: "I will rather have violence than cowardice masquerading as non-violence".

The possessor of a small thumb is easily influenced. He is quickly dominated. He is led by the heart and not the head. He is a man of ideas but not of action.

III

PARTS OF THE THUMB

First Phalanx

   i. When the first phalanx is flat, whether short or long, it indicates calmness of temperament, evenness of mind, and reasonableness of action.

   ii. When the first phalanx is too long, it shows energy risen to despotism.

  iii. When the first phalanx is very short, it shows weakness of will, carelessness and indifference.

   iv. The first phalanx of the weak vacillating Louis XVI was very small.

Second Phalanx

   i. When the second phalanx is "wasp-shaped with the centre slightly concave", it is an indication of brilliant intellect. The subject is quick, sharp and deed.

   ii. When the second phalanx is much longer than the first, the subject has a flair for logic and exactitude of reason, but he does not possess sufficient will and determination to carry out his ideas in practice.

Combinations

   i. When the first phalanx is long and the second short, it denotes people who run reckless risks. They lack proper understanding and cannot assess a situation properly. They act in a hurry and repent at leisure.

ii. When the first phalanx is short and the second long, the subject is a practical logician and always in the right in the assessment of everyday situations. His thinking is right but his activity is usually wrong. His actions contradict his ideas.

IV

THE ANGLE OF THUMBS

Right-Angled Thumb

When the thumb stands at right angle to the palm, the subject will brook no opposition. From sheer independence of spirit, his ideas and actions will fly at a tangent, creating centrifugal forces in his conduct, career and character.

The Widely-Outstretched Thumb

A person with a widely-outstretched thumb has great confidence. It adds a factor of certain recklessness to his thoughts and actions. He has a disregard for conventions. When the widely-outstretched thumb is also stiff, the subject can rein his impulses and is not driven away by the steed of his sentiments.

The High-Set Thumb

A man with an extremely small and high-set thumb is closer to the monkey. The thumb of a monkey is very high-set.

Low-Set Thumb

The lower the thumb is set, the higher the natural intelligence. The low-set thumb grows out of the hand nearer the wrist. It is usually a right-angled thumb. It shows a person of strong and independent character. He has a sympathetic nature despite his inclination to fly to the extremes.

Bent-Back Thumb

A bent-back thumb indicates impulsiveness. In the everyday behaviour of such people there is no steadiness of convention or thought-out self-discipline. They are children of nature, sowing wild oats all the time, and morals do not play much part in their lives.

V

TEXTURE OF THE THUMB

The Supple Thumb

The supple-jointed thumb indicates an extravagant nature. The person is free with his mind, money and morals. He is a spendthrift of time, thought and energy, besides money and materials. He is led by his sentiments rather than a practical sense.

The Firm Thumb

Persons with stiff-jointed thumbs are practical people. Cautious and secretive, they advance by slow steps. With a dogged determination they face up the rigours and vigours of life. They have discipline and strong individualities. They are no humdrum day-dreamers.

VI

THE TEXT OF THE THUMB

D. Arpentigy wrote rightly, "The higher animal is revealed in the hand but the man is in the thumb." The entire character and total career of a man can be judged from a proper study of the thumb.

Cramped Thumb

When a well-formed thumb lies down cramped towards the fingers, it indicates a nervous and cautious nature. The subject lacks self-confidence and is too much self-afraid to speak out his mind in the public.

Unequally Developed Thumb

When the thumb is unequally developed and the first phalanx is very large, the subject is a person of his self-will. He carries all before his will. Logic and reasoning are of secondary importance to him.

Phalanx of Passion

When the thumb is rather small and the third phalanx inside the palm is very large, the subject is a constant prey to passion and sexual pleasures and enjoyments.

Waist-Like Thumb

A waist-like thumb indicates tact born of mental powers. The man becomes a great diplomat or a successful go-between or an arbitrator.

Club-Shaped Thumb

A thick club-shaped thumb indicates brutality.
If the club-shaped thumb is thin and flat, it indicates cleverness, subtlety and cunning.

Flexible Thumb

The more flexible the movements of a thumb are, the greater the activity of the mind.

VII

MISCELLANEOUS INDICATIONS

Idiots

Idiots have slightly-developed thumbs.   Usually they keep their hands closed with the fingers above the thumb.

Great Thumbs

Large thumbs are great thumbs. Newton, Voltaire, Leibnitz, Descrates, Galileo, and other great revolutionary thinkers and workers had large thumbs.

Marriage Thumbs

It is best for the marriage partners to have different kinds of thumbs. If the husband has a large thumb, it is best for the wife to have a small one. It may not be good for a husband with a small thumb to marry a woman with a large thumb, because thereby he is launching himself on a long career of henpecked existence.

If both the partners have large thumbs, it will be like a pair of shears. They will cut all that comes between. Each will go his or her way and yet both of them are inextricably interwined.

VIII

THE CHINESE THUMB STUDY

The system of using the thumb-impression instead of the signature in case of the illiterates was first discovered in India, because it was found that no two thumb-impressions are alike.

The Chinese have used thumb impressions for the purpose of divination. It is done by means of the ball of thumb impressed upon a lump of soft wax.

All this is a proof of the eternal fact how much thumb has been considered important in the everyday life of the community in India, China and other countries.

Chapter Ten

NAILS TELL THEIR TALES

The superiority of man is owing to his hands.

—Anaxgoras

The Palmistry of the Nails have had a very great antiquity. Right from the very ancient times the nails have been used in the diagnosis of disease, disaster and death. Thus Milton, one of the greatest poets of the world although no great palmist, indicated: "To have yellow speckles in the nails of one's hands is a great sign of death."

A correct reading, study and observation of nail construction and colour is an invincible index to mental and physical dangers this flesh is heir to. Not only the palmists but even the medical specialists of the Harley Street are looking into nails for the onset of a host of diseases which sweep away millions of people all over the world. The early symptoms of tuberculosis, rheumatism, diabetes and other diseases can be diagnosed from the nails.

But the tell-tale nails do not merely speak of illness. They also indicate robustness of health, happiness, heartiness and highminded principles of life.

I

SIZE OF NAILS

Short Nails

Short well-formed nails are indications of great critical faculties. Such people love arguments and relish debates.

Controversy is the spice of their life. They are true to Goldsmith's description, "Though Vanquished he can argue still." They never accept defeat in a battle of words.

They are also observant of the minutest details.

Long Nails

The long-nailed people are idealistic and less critical. They have sympathetic understanding of other people's

TENDANCY TO HEART TROUBLE   TENDANCY TOWARDS PARALYSIS

THROAT AFFCTIONS   BRONCHIAL – DELICASY OF LUNGS

DELICASY OF LUNGS SPECIAL WEAKNESS BAD CIRCULATION

difficulties. They have broad visions and see both sides of the medal before formulating their own judgments.

Long and Thin

Long and thin nails are indicative of weak physical nature. They bespeak of internal weak organs and other troubles, such as liver trouble, heart trouble, lung trouble and stomach trouble. They indicate T.B. and other diseases.

Short and Square

A heart disease is indicated by short and square nails.

Short and Wide

Short and wide nails are signs of a domineering and pugnacious personality.

Long Square Nails

When the nails are excessively long and square, these indicate a cold self-centred spirit.

II

TEXTURE OF NAILS

Brittle Nails

Brittle nails indicate langyritis, an inflamed throat, bronchial affections, asthma and catarrh, etc.

Thick and Hard

Thick and hard nails are indicators of cruelty, sadism, unchastity and an animal nature.

Soft Nails

Soft nails indicate weakness and lack of will power.

Hard Nails

Hard nails indicate physical vigour.

III

STRUCTURE OF NAILS

Flat Nails

Small and flat nails show a danger of heart disease. This is particularly correct if the moons on the nail are either invisible or very little visible.

Fluted Nails

Fluted nails show delicacy of the lungs. If the nails are long, wide and curved, it is a great sign of tuberculosis. Small fluted nails show throat troubles.

Filbert Nails

A person of a visionary nature is indicated by long filbert nails. He is a sweet-tempered dreamer building an ivory tower of his own in the rose gardens of other people.

Ribbed Nails

Scrofulla and tuberculosis are indications when the nails are curved, both from top back towards the finger and across the finger.

Shell-Shaped Nails

Triangular and shell-shaped nails, inclined to curve up at the edge, indicate that the subject is suffering from paralysis.

Triangular Nails

Nervous diseases, with a tendency to paralysis, are indicated by triangular and shell-shaped nails, inclined to curve up at the edges.

Wedge-Shaped Nails

Wedge-shaped nails indicate great sensitiveness of spirit.

Almond-Shaped Nails

Almond-shaped nails indicate a gentle spirit. Such persons lack clear perception, courage of conviction and forcefulness of character. They are usually beautiful feminine willows.

Curved Nails

Hard and curved nails indicate ambition and malice.

Pointed Nails

Pointed nails indicate imagination, aesthetic sense, and love of beauty and arts.

IV

COLOUR OF NAILS

Rosy Nails

Rosy nails indicate firmness, health, heartiness, loyalty, optimism, and constancy of purpose.

Red Nails

Red Nails indicate a nervous person, easily irritated by the trifles.

Bluish Nails

Bluish nails indicate a poor circulation of blood.

Pale Nails

When the nails are short, square and pale, they indicate a false, dishonest and cunning person.

V

SIGN ON THE NAILS

Black Spots

According to Battista Porta, "Black Spots" indicate grief and sorrow.

White Marks

"White marks on the thumb" indicate a reciprocated attachment.

Black Spots

"Black spots on the thumb" show crime caused by passion.

Star-Shaped White Mark

According to De Peruccio, "a star-shaped white mark" indicates self-deception, unrequitted love, and a vain worship of things and peoples one loves and cares for.

White Mark on Middle Nail

A white mark on the nail of the middle finger shows a journey.

Black Mark on Middle Nail

A black mark on the nail of the middle finger shows loss of reputation and indignity.

White Mark on Ring Finger Nail

A white mark on the nail indicates honour and wealth.

Black Mark on the Ring Finger Nail

A black mark on the ring finger nail indicates a shadow of the coming sad events.

White Mark on Index Nail

A white mark on the nail of the index finger shows gain and profit.

Black Mark on Index Nail

A black mark on the nail of the index finger shows loss and sorrow.

White Mark on Little Nail

A white mark on the nail of the little finger shows success in commercial enterprises.

Black Mark on Little Nail

A black mark on the nail of little finger indicates a business failure.

VI

NEW NAIL KNOWLEDGE

The scientists agree that nails are formed by the electric fluid inside the body. This is hardened by exposure to the air, says Martini, "thus becoming the kind of intervenery substance between the electric fluid and the human skin and flesh."

Nails change in length, breadth, tone, colour, shape and shade, according to one's mental and bodily conditions. Nails are indicators of both health and disease. Nails improve with health and deteriorate with sickness and disease. Like electric bells, the nails announce the coming of diseases and death. In spells of sickness they also announce the recovery of health long before one is out of the nursing home. If anything goes wrong with the treatment, it is told by the nails. Death is declared by the telltale nails long before the doctor can make up his mind.

Biting of nails indicates that one is irritable and has a bad temperament. He worries too much and is rather childish in his behaviour.

Spinal trouble is indicated by narrow, curved and long nails.

Specks on the nails are caused by nervous stress and strain. After mental sickness or physical illness specks appear on the nails. Mental troubles, excitability and nervous breakdown is indicated by nails covered over by specks.

Good nails indicate good spirit and refinement. These are glossy and white, long, transparent, and not brittle. They are of normal character.

Large moons on the nail indicate good circulation of blood.

Chapter Eleven

MOUNTING A STARRY CAREER

Hitch your wagon to a star.

—Emerson

Palmistry comes closest to Astrology in the study of the Mounts on the hand. And that is neither new nor strange. The occult saying is "As above, so below". Every atom is a complete solar system with all the planets. Why the man himself should not be the replica of the universe? There is an ocean in the drop, as there is a drop in the ocean. Little wonder, there are stars in the hands of a man. And these determine our careers. The world is one united whole, obeying the Laws of Unity and Uniformity of Nature. Thus Bulwer Lytton has it in **Zanoni:**

"Nay, it was not precisely of spirits that I spoke; but there may be forms of matter as invisible and impalpable to us as the animalculae in the air we breathe—in the water that plays in yonder basin. Such beings may have passions and powers like our own,—as the animalculae to which I compare them. The monster that lives and dies in a drop of water— carnivorous, insatiable, subsisting on creatures minuter than himself—is not less deadly in his wrath, less ferocious in his nature, than the tiger of the desert. There may be things around us that would be dangerous and hostile to men, if Providence had not placed a wall between them and us, merely by different modifications of matter."

I

MOUNTS IN YOUR PALM!

A human being is a replica of the cosmos. If men
live in the palm of the mountains, the mountains too live
in the palms of men. There are eight mounts on the
human hand:—

    I. The Mount of Jupiter
        —Below the Index finger.

    II. The Mount of Saturn
        —Below the Middle Finger.

    III. The Mount of Apollo
        —Below the Ring Finger.

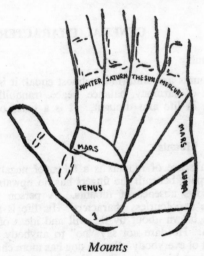

Mounts

   IV. The Mount of Mercury
           —Below the Little Finger
    V. The Mount of Venus
           —Below the thumb.
   VI. The Mount of the Moon
           —Opposite the Mount of Venus,
            towards the wrist side.
 VII. The Upper Mount of Mars
           —Between the Mount of Mercury
            and the Mount of Moon.
VIII. The Lower Mount of Mars
           —Below the Mount of Jupiter.

II

GENERAL CHARACTERISTICS

Equal Mounts

If the mounts are uniform or almost equal, it is a welcome token of harmony, balance, peace, tranquillity and equilibrium in life and thought. It is a hand of peace and plenty.

Absence of Mounts

A total absence of mounts is a token of negative life. When the space beneath the fingers has no upward rising flesh, it shows absence of mounts. A person without mounts has a colourless character. His life is a driftwood to be blown about by the will and ideas of others around him. He dare not say "no" to anybody. He is a Yes—man of everybody. Even a dog has more character. He will follow his master through thick and thin.   A mountless man won't. He is a purchasable commodity like a prostitute. Such people make good mercenaries because they have no pricks of conscience. They can be depended upon only temporarily while you hold them in awe by the will or wealth. They worship the rising sun. For them the slogan is: 'The King is dead! Long live the King!'

Most of the people in the world are of this category. They make the mob. Any aspiring politician has to win them over by persuasion or money. The former is cheaper. They can be persuaded temporarily to follow anybody. They owe mental allegiance to nobody. They are yours while you hold them in pay or persuasion. But their memories are short. Every fifth year they are driven to polls by a demagogue and then quite forgotten for four years. They never care to remember whether the promises made five years back were fulfilled or not. All they are looking for is a new temporary excitement, a new bottle of political whiskey, to drown their everyday difficulties. A tasteful lie waters their mouth. The bigger the lie, the more easily it is believed.

Astrological Palmistry

These mounts belong to what may be called Astrological Palmistry. These are named after the stars of the Solar System, and they exert a starry influence.

These cushion-like developments at the base of fingers and along the edges of the hand play a great role in the determination of your character and career. These pads of flesh indicate the starry influence on the life of a man.

Alice Denton Jennings writes in **Your Hand Tell All:-**

"Any one Mount, that is more highly developed than the others gives a key to the nature of the individual. This main mount must often be considered with an auxiliary mount. By this is meant, where there are two or three mounts of about the same size or development, the meaning of each mount must be analysed, synthesized, and deductions drawn. It must be understood that only in this manner may a hand be placed in its proper category and intelligent deductions arrived at."

Starry Influences

These Mounts exercise a starry influence on your life and happiness. As Comte C. De Saint Germain puts it:—

"Palmistry, cheiromany, cheirosophy, call it what you like, has been said to trace its mysteries to the stars, their influence on the earth and its denizens, the magnetic fluid that incontestably issues from their faraway splendour."

More Important than Lines

There are palmists who consider Mounts more important than lines in the general determination of career and character. They play a great part in the correct assessment of possibilities and potentialities. The right method is that we should combine both the readings of the lines and the observations of the mounts for the right judgment.

"Palmistry", as Mercury says, "is science that weighs up the various qualities and a final result is found by striking a balance of all the individual conclusions."

Chapter Twelve

THE CHARACTER KEY TO CAREER

The palm constitutes five-ninths of the inner surface. In greater or lesser proportion the Mounts occupy space, to this degree the man is said to belong to this Type.

—Alice Denton Jennings

The Mount which predominates all mounts on the palm of your hand determines the type of character to which you belong. The character-types of men and women are classified and catalogued according to the predominant mount on the hand.

A hand-analyst works like a sculptor. A palmist samples hands as a sculptor samples faces. Hand models like face models have to be carefully considered. Men and women are classified according to the predominant mount on their hand. Thus seven mounts give rise to seven types. And for this there is an ancient philosophical basis. Thus writes Rita Van Allen in **You and Your Hand:**—

"There is an age-old theory that in the beginning all humanity was divided into seven parts, and each part was made up of individuals of a distinct type. The habits and attributes, and even the physical appearance of each person in a typical group were alike."

One wonders if it is an historical fact, but at any rate it is a good fancy work: that men of one character should have the same appearance! If that could happen, no person dare be a criminal. And yet on the mental and intellectual plane, all criminals have similar texts and textures.

The Mount Types, originally very much alike, are said to have disappeared due to intermingling caused by marriages, and so now it is not possible to have exact types. Yet there is a controlling element in each of us which belongs to the type of the predominant Mount. Each mount represents distinct type of character.

The analysis of the Mounts is the first thing with which one should start on a trip of investigation in the great mysterious land of characterization. It requires long experience for the correct assessment of character.

When the Mounts are unusually pronounced, like little hills of flesh, they should be carefully noted. They are an obsession and lead to the development of morbid characteristics of the Mount in the subject.

When the mounts are deeply pink, they denote an excess of energy. They also show a great deal of magnetic qualities. Such people are impulsive and headstrong. They needs brakes to their headlong career. They have an inner urge to find expression in activity. Unless they are reined and restrained, willy nilly they go off on a wild-goose chase, sowing wild oats and reaping whirlwinds.

"In the majority of hands, one mount will stand out above the rest. It will be firmer, deeper in colour and higher in bulge. There may be two that appear equally developed. In that case, or in order to decide which mount is stronger, look for colour again, and consistency, and also the length of the finger above it, which may be unusual. And look also for a single deep line, on the mount, for it gives prominence. Once you succeed in correctly estimating a mount-type, a picture of his tendencies and traits unfolds before you."

I

THE JUPITERIAN TYPE

Jupiter is a sign and symbol of vaulting ambition. The Jupiterian Type is a very ambitious man. He is gay, cheerful and optimistic. He is self-confident and fundamentally honest. He is strong and well-built. He is ambitious with an idealistic attitude.

The Jupiterian Type has expressive eyes, a straight nose, and heavy upper lips. He has pride and dignity. He is a warm and sincere lover. He likes wines and seasoned foods. His marriage is usually happy and succesful.

The Jupiterians are born to command and control. They make excellent leaders in politics, business, commerce and society. They are good military generals and business managers. They are big business bosses, company directors and industrial tycoons. As they can pose all the phases of this passing show of life, they make good producers, film directors and actors.

II

THE SATURNIAN TYPE

The Saturnian Type is a great thinker and a philosopher. He shuns mob society and is of reserved nature. He is a born thinker. Habitually he is a recluse and a born cynic.

In physique he is the tallest of the seven types. He has a long face studded with deep-set eyes, heavy eyebrows, and dark hair on the head. His hands have long fingers and his fingers have knots. He has a large mouth and a prominent chin.

His calm contemplative character is a brake on impulsiveness. Therefore, he is the "balance wheel" of all the types. He likes the sad and serious side of things. His philosophy is that of Shri Krishna's "disinterestedness".

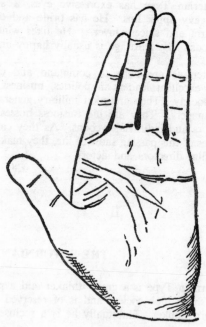

The Saturnian Type

He loves Nature and so agriculture comes home to him. Away from the madding crowd he passes his time in the company of plants and flowers.

Thomas Hardy was Saturnian. He was perpetually sad. Sadness drips from the gloomy novels. So were the great poets of the world like Milton, Shelley, Keats and others. Abraham Lincoln too was in this category. Shakespeare did not belong to this class and was perhaps Jupiterian.

III

THE APOLLOIAN TYPE

The Apolloian Type of man is cheerful and optimistic notwithstanding all rebuffs of fate and fortune. He is healthy and hearty. He gives love for love, twice by the weight, and is thoroughly loveable and amiable.

In physique he is of medium height. He has a white skin, a fascinating face, and beautiful hair. He has almond eyes, a musical voice, and a dancing gait.

His greatest characteristic is love of beauty. He loves painting, music and dance. He is artistic through and through. He lives in poetry and poetry lives in him. He is extremely entertaining and a colourful life dominates him.

Men from all walks of life can belong to the Apollo Type. Many actors are in this category but not all of them. Greta Garbo is too serious to be an Apolloian. Nor can Charlie Chaplin be in this category, because his humour is serious. Mickey Rooney and Shirley Temple did belong to this category. Raj Kapoor is Apolloian but Prithiv Raj Kapoor is Jupiterian.

Mr. Jawaharlal Nehru too belongs to this class.

IV

THE MERCURIAN TYPE

The Mercurian Men are mercurial. They are quick, active and very shrewd in business affairs. They are difficult to deal with in money matters. They love big schemes and big enterprises. Small business does not interest them.

The Mercurian person has an oval face. He has olive skin and dark eyes. He is quick in movement and catches time by the forelock. Outwardly he wears an idle appearance but he lies in wait for his opportunities.

He is short-statured but his body is well-formed. He is gifted with unusual tact. To accomplish his ends he brings his total resources into play. He is fond of smart and fashionable women. Essentially a business-minded being, he knows how to make money and how to save it. Sex for him is a form of amusement. He loves travel, adventure and change of scene.

V

THE VENUSIAN TYPE

The Venusian Type is romantic by nature. He has a graceful form and features. He is fond of fashion, music and dance. He is a voluptuous type and extremely feminine.

The Venusian Type has lush hair and bright round eyes. His body is shapely and well-proportioned. His limbs are graceful. His voice is musical. He has altogether a magnetic personality. He is the great fascinator. He is warm, romantic and attractive. Like bees to a honey-pot, people come to him. He has an aura of fascination.

But sex is not the end for him. It is a via media. He spins up to a higher life round the wheel of sexual energy.

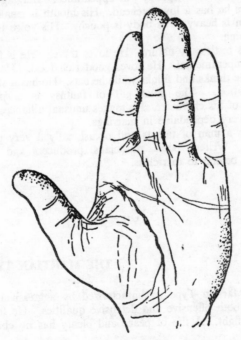

The Mercurian Type

VI

THE LUNARIAN TYPE

The Lunarian Type is a dreamy child of imagination. Away from the madding crowd he loves daydreaming and beauties of nature. The rustling of leaves and singing of birds have a special fascination for him.

He is fat and "spongy" in appearance. Bulging over his eyes he has a low forehead. His mouth is small and his chin is heavy. His body is pouchy. His voice is pitched high.

He is restless by nature. He loves travel. He is fickle and temperamental. He loves good rich food. He eats while he thinks and thinks while he eats. He has a strong imagination. The great gift of fantasy is a special feature of his character. He makes unusual alliances and is not very dependable in marriage.

He is a man of talents and occasionally a very great genius. Writers, poets, musicians, producers and dramatists belong to this class.

VII

THE MARTIAN TYPE

The Martian Type is characterized by aggressiveness. He has both offensive and defensive qualities. He loves a good fight. A life of peace and plenty has no charm for him.

In appearance he is of medium height. He is strongly built. He carries himself with dignity. He has a round face, a small head and a thick neck. He has heavy under-lips and auburn hair. His hand is broad and his palm is pink. His thumb is of aggressive character.

The Martian is out and out a materialist. He would drink life to its lees. Enjoyment after death has no fasci-nation for him. For him a bird in hand is worth four in the bush. He eats well and enjoys good health. He finds the keenest delight in the company of the opposite sex. His potent weapon is vital energy rather than sexual appeal. To attract the opposite sex, like a moth to the flame, he outspreads his peacock feathers of vitality, vanity and wealth.

Chapter Thirteen

THE DOUBLE-CHARACTERED CAREER

"I can choose my own career, to which commonplace society is not essential. I can owe the respect of the world to my art, and not to the accidents of birth and fortune."

"That is, you still persist in your second folly—the absurd ambition of daubing canvass. Heaven forbid I should say anything against the laudable industry of one who follows such a profession for the sake of subsistence; but with means and connexions that will raise you in life, why voluntarily sink into a mere artist? As an accomplishment in leisure moments, it is all very well in its way; but as the occupation of existence, it is a frenzy."

—Bulwer Lytton

Sometimes it is not one Mount that predominates the character of an individual but rather two Mounts are equally predominant. In such individuals new strains of fate and fortune come into existence, some of which are mentioned below.

I

THE JUPITER GIANTS

Jupiter and Saturn

When the Mounts of Jupiter and Saturn predominate the palm, it is a sign of great fortune throughout the life, promising peace, plenty and prosperity, health, happiness, heartiness and home.

Jupiter and Apollo

When Jupiter and Apollo are predominant, it is a good prognostic of wealth and reputation, name and fame, prosperity with honour and social distinction.

Jupiter and Mercury

When the Mounts of Jupiter and Mercury predominate, it indicates a love of scientific research, mathematics, and exact science.

If the combination is accompanied by bad lines, it shows immorality, selfishness and vanity.

Jupiter and Venus

A predominant combination of the Mounts of Jupiter and Venus predicts a pleasant and cheerful disposition. It bespeaks of generosity and honesty. It is also a sign of chivalry.

Jupiter and Moon

A predominance of the Mounts of Jupiter and Moon indicates a sober and quiet disposition.

Jupiter and Mars

When Jupiter and Mars over-reach all others, the indications are courage and self-confidence. For a military career this is a very welcome sign.

II

SATURN STALWARTS

Saturn and Apollo

A Saturn-Apollo predominance indicates a good heart and an exquisite taste.

When accompanied by bad lines, the characteristics are reversed and then it indicates a bad heart and a bad taste.

Saturn and Mercury

A Saturn-Mercury predominance of the palm indicates a desire for scientific knowledge, particularly of medical science. It is essentially a scientist's hand.

Saturn and Venus

A Saturn-Venus predominance is an indication of fondness for occult science, spiritual knowledge and hidden lore.

Saturn and Moon

A Saturn-Moon predominance indicates a love for the mysterious, the unknown, poetry and occult knowledge; and proficiency in the hidden arts.

Saturn and Mars

A Saturn-Mars predominance is a sign of aggressiveness and choleric temper. Combativeness and a domineering spirit are indicated. The person is reckless and a devil-may-care type. He is also a cynic by nature.

III

APOLLO ATHLETES

Apollo and Mercury

An Apollo-Mercury combination of predominance shows eloquence and firmness of purpose. It is an excellent sign for a politician.

Apollo and Venus

An Apollo-Venus predominance indicates an intense desire to please others. Excessive predominance indicates a taste for false flattery.

Apollo and Moon

An Apollo-Moon twin predominant combination is the most powerful sign. It indicates healthy imagination and strong commonsense. The subject has a pure unsophisticated heart.

Apollo and Mars

An Apollo-Mars predominance indicates great love for intellectual pursuits. The subject is a great poet or prose-writer. He is a famous man of letters who has little interest in anything else.

IV

MERCURY MATES

Mercury and Venus

A Mercury-Venus predominance of all mounts indicates a good and affectionate disposition, if other signs are good.

If other signs are bad, it shows fickleness and an ill-balanced mind.

Mercury and Moon

A Mercury-Moon axis indicates a great talent for speculation. If other lines are not favourable, it shows dishonest designs to rob others.

Mercury and Mars

A Mercury-Mars axis is the hand of a strategist and a tactician. He has a quickness of imagination and promptitude of understanding. With bad lines, it shows a double-dealing character.

V

VENUS VICTORS

Venus and Moon

A Venus-Moon axis is an indication of romantic love affair. It shows tendency to elopement. If the Line of Heart is not good, it shows flirtation and inconstancy.

Venus and Mars

A Venus-Mars axis shows a love of the fine arts, painting, music and dancing. In military generals these indicate a desire for quick conquests, the blitz methods of attack.

VI

MOON MARS MAN

The Moon-Mars predominance indicates a great love for navigation. In a bad hand these become a wildgoose chase.

Chapter Fourteen

FROM MOUNTS TO MINDS

If the mountain won't come to Mohammed, Mohammed must go to the mountain.

—English Proverb

The Mounts of Man are Meaningful Mountains of Mystery. Each Mount on your palm has something to teach you, and it can become the Iron Key to unlock the Golden Gates of your character and career.

I

JOYS OF JUPITER

i. Normal growth of the Mount—ambition, honour, love of Nature, spiritual ideas.
ii. Absence of the Mount—lack of respect for parents and elders; raw vulgar instinct.
iii. Excessive development—domineering spirit, arrogance, love of self-publicity.
iv. Predominance of the Mount—exaggerated self-assertion and fondness for flattery.
v. Mount of Jupiter leaning towards Mount of Saturn—love for philosophy, theology and serious study in general.

II

SOUL OF SATURN

i. The Normally-developed Mount—sensitiveness and love of solitude.

ii. Absence of the Mount—life of no importance, vegetative existence.

iii. The Mount normally predominant—failure, frustration and futility, love of music and literature.

iv. Exaggerated Mount of Saturn—dangerous morbidness and tendency to suicide.

v. The Mount of Saturn leaning to the Mount of Apollo—literary success in philosophy, sad poetry, pessimistic novels like Thomas Hardy's.

III

ALTRUISM OF APOLLO

i. Normal Mount of Apollo—success, fame and wealth through arts and literature; physical beauty, generosity and self-confidence; love of self-adornment; affectionate nature.

ii. Absence of the Mount—dull intellect and poor intellectual life.

iii. Slightly developed Mount—love of the beautiful, music and dance.

iv. Exaggerated Mount of Apollo—vanity; love of flattery; jealousy; extravagance.

IV

MERCURY MINDS

i. Normal Mount—business aptitude and fondness of exact sciences; success in business.

ii. Absence of the Mount—lack of business sense; want of intelligence in business affairs.

iii. Exaggerated Mount of Mercury—business dishonesty, deceit and treachery.

iv. When Mercury leans towards Apollo—promise of success in business affairs dealing with arts, science and literature. This is an excellent sign for a publisher.

V

VITALITY OF VENUS

i. Normal Mount of Venus—tenderness for all; love for the beautiful; sincere affection; fondness for music and dancing.

ii. Absence of the Mount—coldness of feelings; lack of interest in beauty, art and Nature.

iii. Exaggerated Mount of Venus—coquetry; extreme selfishness; flirtation; lust.

VI

MOON MOODS

i. Normal Mount of Moon—healthy imagination; love of beauty; music and poetry; love marriage. The Mount is good when close to the wrist.
ii. Absence of the Mount—lack of imagination; dislike for intellectual pursuits.
iii. Exaggerated Mount of Moon—intestinal trouble; billiousness; gout; catarrh.
iv. Predominant Mount—diseased imagination; pessimism; superstition.
v. Narrow and long Mount—resignation and non-violence.

VII

MARS MEN

i. Normal Mount of Mars—courage, self-possession and generosity.
ii. Absent Mount of Mars—timidity and cowardice.
iii. Exaggerated Mount of Mars—violence, aggressiveness, bloodthirstiness.

Chapter Fifteen

CLOUDS ON THE CHARACTER

Every one is as God made him, and often a great deal worse.

—Cervantes

The signs and stars, the dots and dashes, the cuts and crosses on the Mounts greatly make or mar their significance. Some of the important signs are mentioned below.

I

JILTING OF JUPITER

Cross—happy union.
Star—hopeful love affair.
A Star and a Cross—Most brilliant marriage.

One Line—success in business enterprise.
Confused Lines—failure of hopes.

A Spot—misfortune.
Square—protection against misfortune.
Circle—good fortune.

Grill—overwhelming ambition.
Triangle—success in politics.

II

SAILING OF SATURN

Cross—sterility.

Grill—success uncertain.

Spot—Evil influence.

One Line—great success.

Many Lines—no great success.

Many Lines falling towards the Line of Heart—rheumatism.

Star—death by violence.

Square—safety against death by violence.

Triangle—occult powers.

III

ATOP OF APOLLO

Star—riches.

Star with several small lines—sure sign of wealth.

Star with a good Apollo Line—distinction in life.

Grill—great conceit.

Cross—failure in artistic work.

Spot—ignominy.

One Line—fame and riches.

Circle—fame.

Triangle—carefulness.

Square—protection aganist failure.

IV

MYSTERY OF MERCURY

One Line—unexpected good luck.
One single crossed line—loss through stealing.
Three Lines—sign of a good doctor or druggist.
Many confused lines—confused business interests.

Star—thievery and deceit.
Spot—trouble in business.
Grill—death due to accident.
Cross—diplomacy and deception.

Triangle—cleverness in business.

V

WORKS OF VENUS

Star—death of the loved one.
Square—imprisonment due to passion.
Triangle—cold calculations in love affairs.
Grill—love of curiosity.

Cross—unhappy love affair; curiosity of love.
Spot—desertion by the loved one.
One Line—happy combination.
Several Lines—dependence on others.
Confused Lines—passionate temperament.

VI

MAGNIFICENCE OF MOON

One Line—coming danger.
Many lines—dreaminess; fickleness in love.
Cross—sentimental nature.
Grill—discontented nature; morbid gloominess.

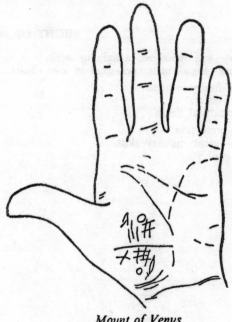

Mount of Venus

Triangle—a cold calculating nature.
Star—death by water, in a journey.
Circle—death by water.
Square—safety against danger.

Spot—nervous trouble.

VII

MIGHT OF MARS

One Line—aggressiveness; a fighting spirit.
Two Lines—a violent temperament in love affairs.

Star—self-injury in anger.
Circle—disaster.
Grill—unnatural death.

Square—protection.
Triangle—great military skill.

Chapter Sixteen

THE ROADS TO YOUR CAREER!

Today it is a fact proved by the discovery of scientific men that each brain cell is an electric dynamo, and energy generated by thought has been recorded on graphs.

—William C. Benham

Are the lines on the hand chaotic or arbitrary? No! They follow the laws which have been tested by time and confirmed by the scientific palmists as well as palmistry-minded scientists. Not all palmists are unscientific. And not all scientists are anti-palmists. Inside the heart of every human being there is an awe of the hidden future which casts a ghastly shadow on the golden page of the book of the present. Here are some observations from a famous Master of Occult:—

   i. 'In the peaceful happiness of that day, the philosopher will carry about with him, not the elixir, but the poison.'

  ii. 'We love the beautiful and serene, but we have a feeling as deep as love for the terrible and dark'.

A proper study of the Lines on the hand can offer you the necessary physical and psychological protection against the Fears of the Unknown and smoothen your path to success. As Cheiro declares:

"To be able to read the hand is to be able to read the secret book of nature, that volume whose pages are human Life and Death, and whose clasp is the golden thread of hope that runs through all men's lives."

I

INDEX TO PERSONALITY

The Lines on your hand are the index to your personality. By studying them carefully you know what pitfalls to avoid and where to find the Rosy Royal Road in a meadow beset with thorns and thistles. Every line on the hand must be carefully depicted on the screen of your mind and deciphered. As Josef Ronald declares:—

"Eminent psychologists and physiologists the world over agree that, along the convulsions of the brain, the lines in the palm of the hand serve as index to the personality of every man, woman and child."

II

HOW TO STUDY THE HAND

In the case of men the right hand is considered more important than the left hand. In the case of women the left hand is considered more important than the right hand.

The right policy is to study both the hands before arriving at a judgment. In the case of men the left hand shows the hereditary qualities, while in the case of women the hereditary qualities are indicated by the right hand.

In the case of men the right hand shows the development of career and character (which is shown by the left hand in the case of women) over and above the abilities and capabilities inherited from the parents. If there is no improvement it shows that the man has made no effort to improve his mental and physical perspective and prospects. If there is a deterioration, it is very regrettable because the person has lost even the jewels of character he inherited from his parents.

Two Spheres of Influence

According to Cheiro the hand is divided into two hemispheres of character-study:—

"The hemisphere, containing the fingers and Mounts of Jupiter, Saturn, Sun (Apollo), Mercury and Mars, representing the mind, and the lower, containing the base of the hand, representing the material.

"It will thus be seen that with this clear point as a guide the student will at once gain an insight into the character of the subject under examination.

"This division has hitherto been ignored but it is infallible in its accuracy."

III

STUDIOUS STUDY

The lines of a hand should be studied by a student studiously. The geographer of the career and character must investigate the map of the hand with full concentration of mind. He must call both logic and patience into play to bring forth the best in his subject, to help him brighten his prospects and to save him from stumbling in the pitfalls of faults and foibles.

Draw balanced and well-thought-out conclusions on the basis of the total survey of the hand-map. You are not bound by the opinions and ideas of this palmist or that. You can pioneer your own reasonable rosy royal roads to prophecy and prediction. For example, it is not necessary that the lady's left hand is necessarily the best hand. I have found cases, on the basis of experience and observation, in which the right hand did give better conclusions about what was already known about the subject's past and present. So I advise that both the hands should be studied and given almost equal weight for the drawing of final conclusions.

Do Lines Change?

Yes, lines do change **slightly** almost every seven years to mark the changes that have been brought about in the career of the subject on the basis of changes in his character. But these changes only take place when a person has made a genuine effort to brighten his prospects in life. If no attempt has been made, or only an half-hearted attempt has been undertaken, or any attempt to change the deeply-grounded habits has ended in failure and frustration, no change is indicated in the lines. On the contrary, if the character of a person has degenerated and has early promise has been nipped in the bud, the consequent worsening of the psychological situation is faithfully recorded on the graph of the hand.

William G. Benham has squintly expressed himself on this point in his book **The Laws of Scientific Hand Reading:**—

"People do not change their typical qualities until they have a strong desire to change and are armed with a firm resolution to do so. Thus it will be seen that there is no greater truth than that we are indeed free agents, planned for a pre-arranged destiny but always able to change it if we determinedly desire to do so.

"There is indeed no such thing as absolute fatalism even though we have so strong an indication in that direction from the seven types. The statement, 'The Lord helps him who helps himself' applies."

Chapter Seventeen

THE LINES OF CAREER AND CHARACTER

Everything from a snow flake to a nation has a design, a plan—call it Destiny if you will. And, so has your life. With a study of the hand, the form of your life's design can be reasonably traced.

The basic design herein drawn is like a bare young tree. The branches and leaves, the blossoms and fruit, are the efflorescence that you, yourself, create, cultivate and increase, through your way of living, your inclinations and your self-direction.

—Rita Van Alen

The human hand is covered with lines—big and small, visible and invisible. Some of the lines are so minute that these cannot be observed by the naked eyes. All lines have a tale to tell. Every line hides a vital code of character. Not even the greatest palmist can explain significance of every line on the palm of a human hand. If we could fully grip and grasp the meaningful mystery of the lines on a single human hand, we shall be able to guide and predict not merely the career and character of a single individual, but rather the career and character of the entire universe, because every human hand is a microcosm of the macrocosm.

It being impossible to study all the lines on a human hand, we naturally concentrate on important lines only. Some of the men and women have too many lines on their hands and some of them have too few; but there are a number of lines which most of the people have more or less in common among them. These are the lines by which we pilot the ship of career and character.

Scientific Explanation

Balzac has given us the scientific explanation of the mysterious lines on the hand:—

"When one thinks that the line separating our flesh from the growing nail contains the unexplainable and invisible mystery of the incessant transformation of our fluid into horn, one must admit that nothing is impossible in the marvellous transformation of human constituting elements."

Every hand is a tape-recorder and the lines are the graphs which need expert people to decipher them to put the locomotive of a career on its rails. Muller has thus explained this phenomenon:—

"Perhaps there exists between the phenomenon of the nervous system and of electricity a sympathy of connection at present unknown, analogous to that which has been found to exist between electricity and magnetism."

I

PRINCIPAL LINES

The Principal Lines on the hand, which are the great determining factors, in character and career, are the following:—

1. **Line of Life**

The Line of Life girdles around the Mount of Venus, at the base of the thumb. This is the most important line on the hand. It should be clear, straight and deep. Any cut, break, cross or any other sign is usually a bad omen. A break always signifies a death.

2. Line of Head

The Line of Head starts close to the Line of Life, between the thumb and the Index Finger, and runs across the palm, dividing it almost into two hemispheres. The straight line shows hard-headed materialism. The curved line shows spiritualism, philosophy and art. The signs on the Head Line alter significances.

3. Line of Heart

Line of Heart starts from the Mount of Jupiter and runs across the hand above the Line of Head, almost bisecting the upper hemisphere of the hand.

4. Line of Fate

The Line of Fate starts from the wrist and goes up vertically, crossing the lines of Head and Heart, running opposite the Line of Life. In some cases the line stops short near the Head or Heart Line. In many cases it is completely missing, showing lack of good fortune.

5. The Line of Apollo

The Line of Apollo runs round the Mount of Apollo at the base of the Ring Finger. It is also called the Line of Sun or the Line of Brilliancy. It indicates literary fame and social distinction.

6. The Line of Marriage

The Line of Marriage is on the side of the hand, close to the Mount of Mercury under the little finger.

It is a little line but it means much to most of the people.

7. The Girdle of Venus

The Girdle of Venus is round the Mounts of Apollo and Saturn round the bases of the Middle Finger and the Ring Finger. This line, not to be found on all hands, shows sensitivity and occult powers.

II

SUBORDINATE LINES

The Subordinate Lines on the hand are the following:—

i. Lines of Travel

These lines are found on the side of the hand, close to the Mount of the Moon, under the Line of Head's end.

ii. The Milky Way

This line runs across the Mount of Moon. It is also called Via Lasciva or Cephalic Line.

iii. The Line of Liver

The Line of Liver runs close to the Line of Fate, on the Mount of the Moon, and above towards or across the Lines of Head and/or Heart. It is also known as Hepatica or the Line of Health.

iv. The Line of Mars

The Line of Mars is the sister line of the Line of Life and runs parallel to it across the Mount of Venus at the base of the Thumb.

v. The Line of Intuition

It is also known as the Line of Moon or Luna. It runs on the Mount of Moon, near it or across it.

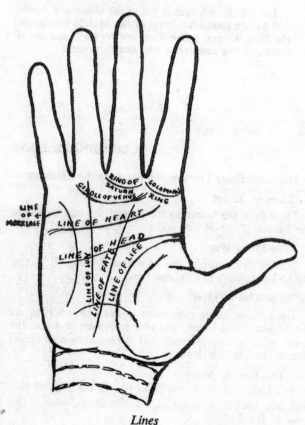

Lines

vi. The Rascette

The three Bracelets or Rascette are three lines on the wrist, at the base of the hand, just below the Line of Life.

III

SUBSIDIARY LINES

The Subsidiary Lines are found everywhere on the palm. They counterbalance and neutralize the character-code of principal and subsidiary lines. These are important subsidiary lines:—

A. Lines on the Thumb

The Lines on the thumb should be considered along with other indications of the thumb for a proper assessment of character.

B. Lines on the Fingers

There are plenty of tiny lines on the fingers and these are meaningful to expert scientific palmists.

C. Lines on the Mounts

All lines, crosses, stars, and spots on the Mounts are meaningful. These have already been dealt with in Chapter Fourteen.

D. Ascending Line

An Ascending Line on a principal or subordinate line shows ascending influence and should be considered good.

E. Descending Line

A Descending Line on a principal or subordinate line shows descending influence and should be considered bad.

IV

FIRST KNOW THYSELF

Palmistry is a science of First-Know-Thyself. Great mysteries are hidden inside the man, and palmistry helps him unravel those secrets. As Alice Denton Jennings says, "Palmistry is a science, which in its highest and truest conception has its aim the motto of ancients 'Know Thyself', the simplest but grandest sermon that can ring in human ears."

If the superiority of a hand is indicated by its lines, "the superiority of man", says Anaxagoras, the great Greek philosopher, "is owing to his hands." The man is as his hands are. The hands are the man. Vehicular wheels have made the use of legs less necessary but no mechanical instrument can replace the human hands.

"Why should not the hand", says Balzac rightly, "give the characteristics of man's physiognomy, since the hand is the medium of manifestation of human action?"

The human hand is a magnificent piece of mysterious mechanism which has baffled the scientists for centuries. "In the hand", says Sir Richard Owen, "every single bone is distinguishable from one another, each digit has its own peculiar character."

All the lines must be carefully considered, weighed and valuated, whether these lines are principal, subordinate or subsidiary, to form and formulate a right judgment. As **Mercury** says, "Palmistry is a science that weighs up the various qualities and a final result is found by striking a balance of all the individual conclusions."

Chapter Eighteen

THE CAREER AND CHARACTER
OF LINES

It would be surprising if all the tests were applied to an individual's hand and they invariably gave the same reading. What usually happens is that one reading partly contradicts the other. This does not mean that Palmistry is a science that weighs up the various qualities and a final result is found by striking a balance of all the individual conclusions.

—Mercury

The lines of career and character are made, modified or marred by the career and character of lines. Two men may be in cars but one's car is the latest model while another's is dated 1943. Both cannot be equal. Two men may be in the same boat, and yet one may sink while the other swims across.

The value of the lines depends upon their clarity, depth, colour, strength, subsidiary lines and other signs. Nor should lines be considered without correlation with the Mounts and the thumb.

"Thumb", says Sir Richard Owen, "which is the least important and constant digit of the anterior extremity of the rest of the animals, becomes in man the most important element segment and that which makes it a hand properly so called."

I

COLOUR AND CHARACTER

Rosy Lines
These lines are the best. They indicate health, hope and highmindedness.

Red Lines
Red lines indicate violence, overflow of energy, impulsiveness, drunkenness.

Yellow Lines
These are indications of billiousness and liver trouble.

Pale Lines
These are indications of sickness and ill health.

Dark Lines
These indicate a proud and melancholy temperament.

White Lines
In a patient these indicate bloodlessness and approaching death.

II

DOUBLE CHARACTER

When a sister line runs parallel to the main line, the qualities indicated by the main line are strengthened. Any break, cross or ill-omen in the main line is bridged over by the sister line. If an ill-omen in the main line is repeated in the sister line, its occurrence becomes a dead certainty. The same is true of good signs on both the lines.

III

LINES OF INFLUENCE

Lines of Ascending Influence

Lines of Ascending Influence are small branches of the main line, going upwards. These are good for the subject.

Lines of Descending Influence

Lines of Descending Influence are small branches of the main line going downwards. These are bad for the subject.

IV

CHARACTER OF LINES

Split Lines

Split lines are not good lines. These indicate an uncertain course of action.

Breaks in Lines

Every break in the line is an indication of the failure of the course and career of the line.

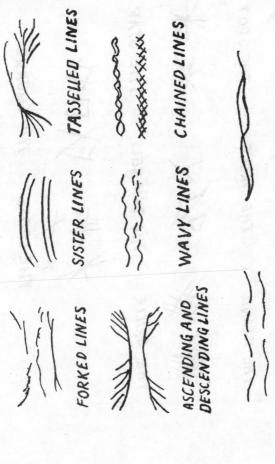

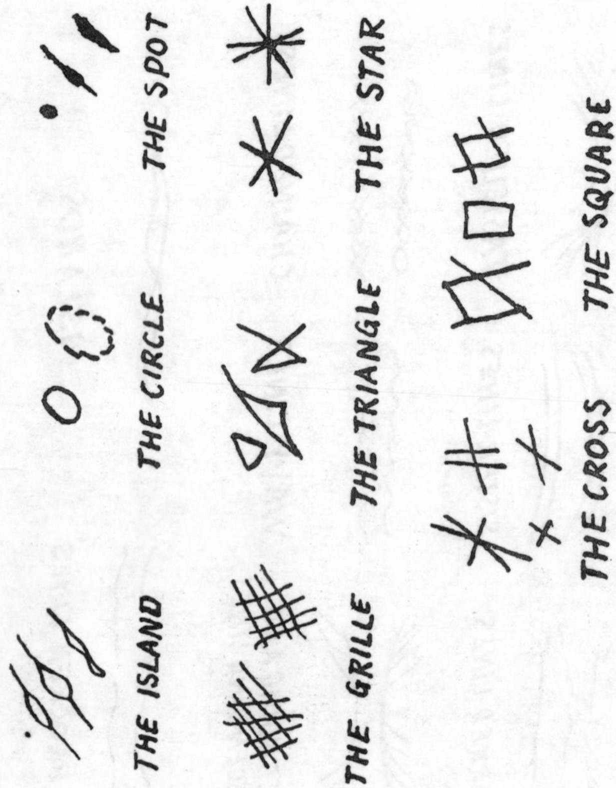
THE ISLAND
THE CIRCLE
THE SPOT
THE GRILLE
THE TRIANGLE
THE STAR
THE CROSS
THE SQUARE

Network of Lines

When the hand is covered with a network of confused lines, it shows a mental confusion and a confused mind.

Chained Formation

A chained formation in any line is a sign of weakness of the course of action indicated by it.

On the Life Line a chained formation indicates a permanent invalid.

On the Head Line it indicates want of intellectual capacity.

On the Heart Line it shows unreliability and unstability of mind.

V

SIGNS ON THE LINES

Cross

It shows an obstacle.

Circle

It is an unusual sign and its value differs in different lines. On Life Line it shows poor eyesight.

Grille

A grille is a number of lines crossing each other at right angles. It is a serious menace.

Triangle

A triangle is a sign of mental brilliance.

Trident

A Trident is a three-pronged spear-head. It is a favourable indication. It adds strength and brilliance. It increases chances of success.

Star

A star may be good or bad according to its location.

Cross-Bar

These are horizontal lines without crosses. These indicate the worst defects.

Square

The square is a favourable sign. It indicates protection against danger. A square near a break in the line offsets any harm indicated by the break.

Dots

Dots point out to defects. Small temporary dots are usual after illness. Big permanent dots are a great menace.

Island

An island shows defect. The extent of defect depends upon the extent of the island.

Tassel

Tassel indicates weakening of power in old age. It shows decay and destruction.

Fork

In case of Life Line it is a bad omen. In other cases it is good.

Chapter Nineteen

LITTLE LIFE-LINE LAWS

How often, crook-trunked tree, she looks to thy green boughs; how often, like thee, in her dreams and fancies, does she struggle for the light;—Not the light of the stage-lamps. Pooh, child! be contented with the lamps, even with the rush-lights. A farthing candle is more convenient for household purposes than the stars.
—Bulwer Lytton

Laws of life are life of laws. How does it profit you if you gain the whole world and lose thyself? With health you can have no career. What is the use of brightening up your opportunities in life when the very ladder you stand upon is snatched from below your feet, and you come tumbling down? What is the fun of having a great career if you shuffle off the mortal coil before you can taste the golden apple?

You must say proper attention to the indications on the Life Line on your palm. Strengthen the good points. Get rid of the vices and uglinesses.

Your Line of Life is your life-line. Your head and heart hang by its tender thread. The Head Line and the Heart Line are subordinate to the Life Line.

I

CHARACTER AND CONSTRUCTION

Length

The longer the Line of Life, the longer the life. The shorter the Life Line, the shorter the life.

Breadth

i. A thin and meagre Life Line denotes ill-health.
ii. A broad and deep Life Line denotes good health.
iii. A broad and shallow Life Line denotes dissipation of energies through worry and overwork.

Thin Termination

A sudden stop terminating the thin line indicates death.

Linked Line

A chained or linked line denotes a weak constitution. Chained under Jupiter indicates bad health in childhood.

Without Parallel Lines

When the Life Line ends without parallel lines, it denotes death at the point of termination.

Break

A break in the line shows illness.
A break in lines of both hands indicates death.

Laddered Line

A laddered life line is a sign of continuous ill health.

II

ASSOCIATED ATTRIBUTES

Long Life

A long life is indicated when the Life Line comes out in a great circle and ends near the Mount of Moon.

Great Success

Great success in life is indicated when the Life Line starts under the Mount of Jupiter.

Life of Logic

When the Life Line is closely connected with the Head Line, it denotes a life guided by prudence and reason.

Violent Death

Violent death is indicated by Life Line getting entangled with Head Line and Heart Line at the start.

Action without Thought

When Life Line is widely separated from the Head Line at the start, it denotes rashness and action without thought. Thought follows the action. The man thinks after the leap.

Thought without Action

When Life Line is entangled with the Head Line for some distance, half an inch or so, at the start, it denotes thought without action. The man goes on thinking always but never does anything. This is a typical Indian hand, because most of our people are characteristically philosophers.

Go-Ahead Spirit

Go-ahead spirit is indicated by a small gap between Life Line and Head Line at the start.

III

LINES OF INFLUENCE

Up To Jupiter

When a branch line rises to the Mount of Jupiter it indicates a great rise in life.

Up to Apollo

When a branch line rises to the Mount of Apollo, it denotes success in literature and arts.

Up to Mercury

When a branch line rises to the Mount of Mercury, it denotes success in business.

Up to Head Line

When a branch line rises to the Head Line, it indicates people who interfere with our ideas.

Up to Marriage Line

When a branch line goes up to the Marriage Line, it indicates divorce.

Up to Mount of Mars

When a branch line rises up to the Mount of Mars, it denotes an unfavourable love attachment.

IV

CUTTING & CROSSING LINES

Cutting Line of Life

When lines of influence cut Life Line, the indication is interference in life from relatives.

Attacking Line of Fate

When influence lines cutting Life Line attack Fate Line, it indicates interference of other people in business affairs.

Cutting Line of Head

When lines of influence from Lfe Line cut through Line of Head, these indicate interference by other people in love affairs.

Cutting Line of Apollo

When branch lines from Life Line cut through Apollo Line, these indicate enemies who spoil position in life by spreading scandals.

V

SIGNS THAT SPEAK

Island

i. Island at the source of Life Line—hereditary disease.

ii. Island in the line—disease.

Fork

i. Fork at the beginning of Life Line—sense of justice and fairplay.

ii. Fork going to Head Line—disloyalty.

iii. Fork in the middle of Life Line—unmistakable warning of diminishing powers.

iv. Fork at the end of Life Line—overwork in old age; poverty; death away from home.

Square

A Head Line broken inside a square—recovery from serious illness.

Tassel

When Life Line is tasselled at the end, it indicates monetary losses in old age.

Cross

i. Cross at the beginning of Life Line—accident in early life.

ii. Cross at the end of life—threat of ill health.

iii. Cross cut by branches—mental infirmity.

Black Spot

Branches from a black spot on the line—nervous trouble.

Bar

A bar across a broken end—preservation from illness.

Circle

A circle on the Life Line—blindness.

Small Cutting Lines

Small rays continually cutting Life Line—continuous ill-health not leading to death.

Chapter Twenty

THE HEADWAY TO YOUR CAREER!

It is of extreme importance in connection with this line that the peculiarities of various types should be borne in mind; as for instance a sloping line of head on a psychic or conic hand is not of half the importance as a sloping line on a square hand.

—Cheiro

"With brains, sir!" replied an artist to the question, "How do you mix your colours?"

The colours of your career too have to be mixed with your brains to bring out the best and the brightest in your life. You must use your brains to go ahead in your life across the thorny meadows of competition.

By a proper study of your Head Line you can find out what pitfalls to avoid, what pitfalls to bridge over, and how to reach the Golden Gate of peace, plenty, prosperity, power and popularity.

I

CHARACTER OF HEAD LINE

Length

i. A long, straight and clear Head Line denotes commonsense.

ii. A long and narrow Head Line denotes energy.

P. E.—6

Width

   i. A weak and narrow Head Line denotes frivolity.

   ii. A pale and broad Head Line shows dull intellect.

   iii. A very poor and narrow Head Line denotes chronic
indigestion.

Faintness

   i. A long faint Head Line shows perfidy.

   ii. A short faint line shows idiocy.

Formed in Islands

When the Head Line is formed in little islands, it shows
tuberculosis.

Waviness

When a Head Line is wavy and rises with a curve, it
denotes insanity.

Breaks

When the Head Line is broken into pieces, it denotes
loss of memory.

Sister Line

A Head Line followed by a sister line denotes wealth
by inheritance.

II

QUADRANGULAR QUALITIES

The Lines of Head and Heart are separated by what
is known as the "Quadrangle".

Narrow Quadrangle

A tortuous Head Line with a narrow Quadrangle denotes dishonesty.

Badly-Formed Quadrangle

A badly formed Quadrangle with the Head Line stretching across the palm denotes avarice.

III

ASSOCIATED ATTRIBUTES

Concentration

A power of concentration is indicated by a well-developed Head Line with good Mounts of Jupiter and Mercury. It gives a great drive for success in politics, business and society.

Headache

Headache is indicated by a chained or linked Head Line.

Idiocy

A poor Head Line with abnormally small thumb.

Consumption

Consumption is indicated by an islanded Head Line with fluted nails.

Brain Fever

When Head Line runs close to Life Line for quite a space, brain fever is indicated.

Energetic Action

Energy is declared when Head Line is not joined to the Life Line.

Rashness

Rashness and tactlessness is indicated when Head Line is widely separated from the Life Line.

Excessive Conceit
Excessive conceit is indicated by a Head Line that rises with a curve around the thumb and goes across the palm.

Insanity
Insanity is shown when Head Line is wavy and rises with a curve.

Fatal Love
When the Head Line slants downward very close to Life Line, fatal love is indicated.

Craftiness
Crafty disposition is indicated when the Head Line slopes and ends in a fork in the Mount of Moon.

Short Life
A short life is shown by a Head Line that ends where it crosses the Fate Line.

Presence of Mind
Presence of mind is assured by a Head Line which is long and clear, ending on the lower Mount of Mars.

Prudence
Prudence is indicated by a Head Line joining the Life Line in a very acute angle.

Sudden Death
Sudden death is indicated when Head Line joins Life Line and Heart Line at the start.

IV

LINES OF INFLUENCE

To Mount of Venus
Lines of Influence reaching out from the Head Line to the Mount of Venus indicate financial troubles.

To the Mount of Jupiter
Lines going from the Head Line to the Mount of Jupiter show a brilliant fortune.

To the Mount of Apollo
Lines going from the Head Line to the Mount of Apollo indicate success in literature and arts.

To the Mount of Mercury
Lines going from the Head Line to the Mount of Mercury indicate success in business.

To the Line of Heart
Lines rising from the Head Line and reaching the Line of Heart without cutting it indicate healthy influences by others. If the Heart Line is cut, the Influences are unhealthy.

From the Rascette
A line rising from the Rascette and going across the Line of Head to the Line of Heart shows success in love and romance.

V

STRIPES AND STARS

Island
An island on the Head Line shows neuralgia and brain trouble.

Fork
On Head Line under the Mount of Saturn—good fortune.

At the end of Head Line on the Mount of Moon—wicked imagination.

Triangle

Close to the Mount of Mercury—success in scientific research.

Cross

A cross on the Head Line shows a grave accident.

Star

A star on Head Line indicates a wound on the Head.

Star and Fork

With a fork at the start and a star at the end, the Head Line shows fatal pride.

VI

SPOTS ON HEAD LINE

White Spots—discoveries.

White spots under Mount of Saturn—success in money matters.

White spots under Mount of Mercury—success in business.

Dark spots—tendency to fever.

Bluish spots—tendency to murder.

Blue spot on discoloured Head Line—Liver trouble.

Red spot—head injury.

Chapter Twenty-One

THE HEARTWAY TO YOUR CAREER!

> My heart's in the Highlands,
> My heart is not here;
> My heart's in the Highlands
> A-chasing the deer.
>
> —Robert Burns

You cannot do anything in the world unless you put your heart in it. "Where your treasure is, there will your heart be also," says the Bible. The converse is also true. Where your heart is, there is your treasure.

You need a very big heart to face up to the exigencies of the present situation in the world. "Some people's hearts", says Douglas Jerrold, "are shrunken in them like dried nuts. You can hear them rattle as they walk."

Be true to your heart. Follow the Inner Urge to realize the best in you and the brightest outside you. Try to be what you are. Do not try to be what you are not lest you regret like Shakespeare's Othello:—

> But I will wear my heart upon my sleeve
> For daws to peck at; I am not what I am.

The Line of Heart runs across the upper portion of the hand at the base of the Mounts of Jupiter, Saturn, Apollo and Mercury. The normal Line of Heart is clear, deep, and pink. It may rise from the Mount of Jupiter, the Mount of Saturn or between the two mounts.

1

WHERE HEART RISES!

i. Above the Mount of Jupiter

When the Heart Line rises above the Mount of Jupiter, it denotes excess of affection and passion, an affectionate passion and a passionate affection.

ii. From the Mount of Jupiter

When the Heart Line rises from the Mount of Jupiter, it assures the highest type of love and devotion.   The subject is strong, firm and reliable in romantic affairs. He is a great and noble-hearted person.   He has a respect and regard for the feelings of others.

iii. Below the Mount of Jupiter

When the Heart Line rises between the Mount of Jupiter and the Mount of Saturn, it combines idealism born of Saturn and passion born of Jupiter.   The love is an ideal passion and a passionate idealism.

iv. From the Mount of Saturn

When the Heart Line rises from the Mount of Saturn, it denotes a very sensual and passionate attachment.   The subject is selfish in love affairs and cannot brook rivalry or competition.

II

CHARACTER OF HEART LINE

Total Absence

If there is no Line of Heart, the person lacks feelings of affection.   The man in sensual without sensitivity or finer feelings of fellowship. He is simply driven by animal passions like a lust-hungry beast.

Double Line of Heart

A Double Line of Heart indicates a great capacity of profound affection. Unrequited, it usually ends in sorrow like Gray's **Elegy.**

Colour of Heart Line

Bright red—great violence of passion.
Pale—indifference to love affairs.
Faded—terrible disappointments in love.
Yellow—liver trouble.
Pale and wide—heart trouble.

Breaks

Breaks in line—disappointments in love.
Break under saturn—loss of beloved through fatality.
Break under Apollo—loss of beloved through pride.
Break under Mercury—loss of beloved through folly.

Size of the Line

Thin and bare of branches—indifference to love affairs.
Thin and bare towards the side of the hand—sterility.
Stretching clear across the hand—blind devotion.
Thin and long—murderous instincts.
Chained Line—flirtation.
Broken—faithlessness.

Situation of the Line

Close to the Head Line—head interferes with heart; intellect chills affection.
High on hand away from all lines—a hard and cold nature.
Drooping towards the Line of Head—unhappiness in love.
Lines of Head, Heart and Life joined—an evil sign.
Starting from third phalanx of first finger—failure in all directions.

Encircling mount of Jupiter—jealousy.
United to Head Line under Saturn—fatal events.
United to Head Line under Mercury—early death.
Many lines cutting Heart Line diagonally—heart and
  liver trouble.

III

LINES OF INFLUENCE

To Line of Life

Branch lines connecting Lines of Life and Heart denote illness caused by sorrow due to disappointed love.

To Line of Head

A line of influence from Heart Line to Head Line without cutting the latter denotes fatal infatuation.

Lines from Heart Line not touching the Head Line
indicate life greatly influenced by the opposite sex.

From the Line of Fate

Short lines ascending from the Fate Line to the Heart
Line denote love not consummating in marriage.

IV

SCARS AND STARS

Island

Island on the Heart Line—adulterous love affairs.

Fork

One fork under the Mount of Jupiter—good fortune.

Three forks under the Mount of Jupiter—very great fortune.

Circle

A circle on the Heart Line shows weakness of heart.

Dot

Under the Mount of Apollo—sentimental grief.

Under the Mount of Mercury—trouble due to a lawyer, a doctor or a scientist.

Red Spot

A red spot on Heart Line indicates possibility of wounds.

Deep Scar

A deep scar across the line indicates danger of apoplexy.

Star

A star on a line of influence ending on the Mount of Moon indicates hereditary madness.

Crosses

Crosses or chains at the junction of the Heart Line and Line of Fate—pecuniary troubles.

Chapter Twenty-Two

THE TREASURE TROVE OF FATHER FORTUNE

There is a tide in the affairs of men
Which, taken at the flood, leads on to fortune.

—Shakespeare

Zanoni made Viola speak to him of her father. He made her recall some of the airs of Pisani's wild music. And these airs seemed to charm and lull him into reverie.

"As music was to the musician", said he, "may science be to the wise. Your father looked abroad in the world; all was discord to the fine sympathies that he felt with the harmonies that daily and nightly sail afloat to the throne of heaven. Life, with its noisy ambition and its mean-passions, is so poor and base! Out of his soul he created the life and the world for which his soul was fitted. Viola, thou art the daughter of that life, and will be the denizen of the earth."

The Line of Fate is the most important line of every student who is out to carve a great career for himself in this sordid world. Out of the mud of poverty and squalor rise the great lotus flowers like Viola. The hand of Father Fortune guides them to the secret treasure troves.

The Line of Fate is also called the Line of Saturn or the Line of Chance. It rises from the wrist and goes vertically up to Jupiter or Saturn.

I

CHARACTER OF FATE LINE

Rising of Fate

i. Rising zigzag or a knot of crosses—trouble in childhood.

ii. Rising from the Mount of Moon—intuition and occult powers.

iii. Rising from the Mount of Moon with many horizontal lines—constant travelling.

iv. Rising from the Line of Head—success late in life.

v. Rising from the Line of Head and circling under the Mount of Saturn—a very hard life.

vi. Rising from the Mount of Moon and reaching the the Mount of Saturn—a very hard life.

Running of Fate

i. Running directly up to the Mount of Apollo—reputation achieved in arts and literature.

ii. Chained while crossing the Line of Heart.—trouble in love affairs.

iii. Wavy and chained Fate Line—unhappiness.

iv. Absence of Fate Line—pointless life.

v. Thick on Mount of Moon, thin on Line of Life—great sentimentality.

vi. Broken Line of Fate—every break denotes a change of career.

Setting of Fate

i. Terminating on Mount of Mercury—great success in business.

ii. Terminating on the Line of Heart—despondency.

iii. Terminating at the Line of Head—misfortunes through mistakes.

II

SCARS AND STARS

Cross

At the termination of the line—misfortune.
On the line—change of career.

Stars

On the line—imminent dangers.
At the termination—death by paralysis.

Island

Island on the line—marriage trouble.

Chapter Twenty-Three

THE LINE OF BRILLIANCY

Training is everything. The peach was once a bitter almond; cauliflower is nothing but cabbage with a college education.

—Mark Twain

Zanoni is the ancient model of a man with a radiant Line of Brilliancy.

They all described Zanoni as a man keenly alive to enjoyment—of manners, the reverse of formal—not precisely gay, but equable, serene and cheerful; ever ready to listen to the talk of others, however idle, or to charm all ears with an inexhaustible fund of anecdotes and worldly experience.

All manners, all nations, all grades of men seemed familiar to him. He was reserved only if allusion were every ventured to his birth of history. The more general opinion of his origin certainly seemed the more plausible.

His riches, his familiarity with the languages of the East, his residence in India, a certain gravity which never deserted his most cheerful and familiar hours, the lustrous darkness of his eye and hair, and even the peculiarities of his shape, in the delicate smallness of the hands, and the Arab-like turn of the stately head, appeared to fix him as belonging to one at least of the Oriental races.

And can you be Zanoni? Yes, you can be Zanoni, even though you do not have his line of Occult Brilliancy. Lines on the hand are not invincible tracks. It does not mean that those who do not have the Line of Brilliancy cannot be brilliant. They can be so with effort. Those who have the Line of Brilliancy are brilliant with natural effortlessness. But even they can lose brilliance, despite their Line of Brilliancy, if they are pushed into unfavourable circumstances, as among the gamblers, drunkards and criminals. Then their brilliance finds an expression in the dice and the house-breaking.

The Line of Brilliancy is a Line of Tendency to be Brilliant. The line is a radiogram of mental and intellectual processes, teleprinted on the hand. As Abercrombie says, "The communication of reception from the senses to the mind has been accounted for by the motions of the nervous fluid, by vibrations of the nerves, and a subtle essence resembling electricity or galvanism."

The Line of Brilliancy, also called the Line of Apollo, or Sun, is found at the base of the Ring Finger, on or near the Mount of Apollo. It is a sister line of the Line of Fate. Both the Lines must be read in conjuction to draw the right conclusions.

Line of Fate and the Line of Brilliancy read jointly prove that all qualities of career and character can be acquired in two ways: either naturally or culturally. If these are not bestowed on you by Mother Nature, you can cultivate them yourself. Fruits and flowers are found in wild nature; but these can also be grown agriculturally. The same is true of your career and character. As Rita Van Alen declares:—

"Everything from a snow flake to a nation has a design, a plan—call it Destiny if you will. And, so has your life. With a study of the hand, the form of your life's design can be reasonably traced. The basic design herein drawn is like a bare young tree. The branches and leaves, the blossoms and fruit, are the efflorescence that you, yourself, create, cultivate and increase, through your way of living, your inclinations and your self-direction."

I

CHARACTER OF THE LINE

Well-Shaped Line

A well-shaped Line of Brilliancy shows sure success.

Long and Uncrossed

When the Line of Brilliancy is long and uncrossed, it shows wealth and riches.

Pale Line

A pale line of Brilliancy shows love and talent for art and literature but not backed for sufficient effort and patience for its realization.

Poorly Formed Line

A poorly formed Line of Brilliancy indicates only a superficial interest for cultural pursuits, like rich men having encyclopaedias lined in their drawing rooms for the purpose of decoration rather than serious study.

Deeply Formed Line

A deeply formed Line of Brilliancy indicates success and reputation through arts and literature.

Tasselled Termination

A tasselled termination of the line near the Mount of Apollo indicates failures.

Broken Line

A line broken repeatedly indicates versatility that brings neither money nor reputation.

Badly Traced Line

A badly-traced line cut up continuously by small lines shows bankruptcy.

II

ASSOCIATED ATTRIBUTES

Talent for Evil

A talent for evil is indicated by a hollow hand, twisted fingers and a long line of Brilliancy.

Great Fame and Honour

Great fame and honour in arts and literature is indicated by a clearly-marked Line of Brilliancy in both hands with a star on the Mount of Apollo.

Great Riches

Great riches are indicated by a narrow, deep and straight and uncrossed Line of Brilliancy that ascends to the Mount of Apollo.

Ambition

Ambition is denoted by a good Line of Brilliancy, a good Line of Fate, and a high Mount of Jupiter.

Gambling Tendencies

Gambling tendencies are indicated by a narrow Line of Brilliancy and a sloping Line of Head.

Loss of Fortune Due to Marriage

Loss of fortune due to marriage is indicated by a line from the Line of Marriage cutting the Line of Brilliancy.

Success of Finance

Success in financial affairs is indicated by a line of influence rising from the Line of Head to the Line of Brilliancy.

Failure From Finance

Failure in arts for want of finance is indicated by a line from the Mount of Saturn cutting the Line of Brilliancy.

Untold Success in Arts
Untold success in arts is indicated by two sister lines, one on either side, of the Line of Brilliancy.

Failure From Fickleness
Failure from fickleness and purposelessness is indicated by a line from the Mount of Mercury cutting the Line of Brilliancy.

Opposition from Rivals
Opposition from rivals is indicated by lines crossing the Line of Brilliancy.

III

SCARS AND STARS

Island
Island indicates danger from heart disease.

Fork
Fork on the Line of Brilliancy indicates fame, riches and reputation.

Cross
A cross indicates a pious disposition.

Black Spot
A black spot indicates danger of blindness.

Trident Terminus
When the Line of Brilliancy terminates in three branches —one pointing towards the Mount of Mercury, one towards the Saturn, and the third on the Mount of Sun, it shows a very great distinction achieved in life and letters.

Chapter Twenty-Four

MARRIAGE MAKES OR MARS MAN

The Hand of a Man
Is the make of his life. . . .
Hang to your old love,
Not hunt a new wife.

— Martini

Benjamin Franklin said that one has three reliable friends in life: an old wife, an old dog and ready money. But to have an old wife you have got to have a young wife first. And then, she must have the opportunity to become old. But who knows? Marriage is a whirlpool full of dangerous crags. There are more chances of your career being shipwrecked than reaching the harbour.

The first and the foremost thing is that you should be true to your partner in thought, word and deed. Marry for love, friendship and happiness. Do not marry for any extraneous considerations.

I

A WIFE FOR YOUR CAREER ONLY!

If you are looking for a diplomatic assignment in the Indian Foreign Service, a handsome wife can advance your prospects in life, but do not behave like the Frenchman Nicot in Zanoni:—

"Do you know the Signora Pisani?   Have you ever spoken to her?"

"Not yet. But when I make up my mind to anything, it is soon done. I am about to return to Paris. They write me word that a handsome wife advances the career of a patriot. The age of prejudice is over. The sublimer virtues begin to be understood. I shall take back the handsomest wife in Europe."

"Be quiet! What are you about?" said Mervale, seizing Glydon, as he saw him advance towards the Frenchman, his eyes sparkling, and his hands clenched.

"Sir!" said Glyndon, between his teeth, "you know not of whom you thus speak. Do you affect to suppose that Viola Pisani would accept you?"

"Not if she could get a better offer", said Mervale, looking up to the ceiling.

"A better offer? You don't understand me," said Nicot. "I, Jean Nicot, propose to marry the girl, marry her! Others may make her more liberal offers, but no one, I apprehend, would make one so honourable. I alone have pity on her friendless situation. Besides, according to the dawning state of things, one will always, in France, be able to get rid of a wife whenever one wishes. We shall have new laws of divorce. Do you imagine that an Italian girl—and in no country in the world are maidens, it seems more chaste (though wives may console themselves with virtues more philosophical)—would refuse the hand of an artist for the settlement of a prince? No; I think better of the Pisani than you do. I shall hasten to introduce myself to her." . . .

"I may offer her marriage as well as yourself."

"That would be folly in you, though wisdom in me. You would not know how to draw profit from the speculation! **Cher confrere,** you have prejudices."

"You do not dare to say you would make profit from your own wife?"

"The virtuous Cato lent his wife to a friend. I love virtue, and I cannot do better than imitate Cato. But to be serious—I do not fear you as a rival. You are good-looking, and I am ugly. You are irresolute, and I am decisive. While you are uttering fine phrases, I say simply, 'I have a bon etat. Will you marry me?' So do your worst, cher confrere. Au revoir, behind the scenes!"

This is how even the ugliest self-confident tricksters walk away with the most beautiful girls in the world and lead them to their doom and the slaughter-house like cattle, while more deserving dilly-dally dandies keep looking on!

II

LINES OF ATTACHMENT

The Lines of Marriage are also called the Lines of Attachment. They are found along the wrist of the hand below the little finger near, below or across the Mount of Mercury.

No Short Love-Affairs Indicated

As Comte C. de Saint-Germain says in **Practical Palmistry,** "It does not refer to short affairs of the heart, but to all such intercourses the duration and the completeness of which are apt to leave absolute and durable marks, at the time upon the nervous system of the subject."

Affection, Not Marriage, Indicated

"It must be first stated, and stated clearly", says Cheiro, "that the hand does not recognise the mere fact of a ceremony, be it civil or religious . . . . it merely registers the influence of different people over our lives, what kind of influence they may have had, the effect produced, and all that is in accordance with such influence."

III

CHARACTER OF THE LINE

Sloping towards Line of Heart

When the Marriage Line slopes towards the Line of Heart, it indicates widowhood.

Broken Line

A broken Marriage Line indicates divorce or separation.

Well-Traced Line

A well-traced Marriage Line indicates happy marriage.

Close to the Line of Heart

If the Marriage Line is close to the Heart Line, it indicates an early marriage between the ages of fourteen and twenty.

Near the Centre of Mercury

If the Marriage Line is found near the centre of the Mount of Mercury, it indicates marriage in the twenties between 21 and 28 years of age.

Up the Mount of Mercury

If the Marriage Line is three-quarters up the Mount of Mercury, it indicates a marriage between 28 and 35.

Upward Curve

When the Marriage Line curves upward, the subject is not likely to marry at all.

Parallel Line

A line running parallel to Marriage Line indicates deep affection after marriage.

IV

ASSOCIATED ATTRIBUTES

Troublesome Marriage Problems

Troublesome marriage problems are indicated by an influence line from the Mount of Venus cutting lines of Marriage, Heart, Head and Life.

Illness of Partner

Illness of marriage partner is indicated by the capillary lines from the Marriage Line towards the Heart Line.

Opposition to Marriage

Opposition to marriage is indicated by a line from the root of the Little Finger cutting the Marriage Line.

Bad Alliance

Bad alliance is indicated by a branch downward touching the Line of Brilliancy.

Marrying High

Marrying a person in high position is indicated by a branch upward towards the Line of Brilliancy.

Capricious Marriage

A capricious marriage with no real attachment is indicated by a line of influence from the Mount of Moon rising to the Marriage Line. If the Influence Line is strong and clearly marked, it indicates a wealthy attachment even though capricious.

Influenced by Partner

When an Influence Line is stronger than the Marriage Line, it shows predominant influence of the marriage partner.

Happiest Marriage Symbol

Happiest marriage symbol is indicated by a Line of Influence running close to the Fate Line.

Obstacles to Marriage

Obstacles to marriage are indicated by a line from the Mount of Mercury cutting through the Marriage Line.

V

SCARS AND STARS

Black spot—widowhood.
Drooping with a cross—death of marriage partner.
Island—matrimonial trouble.
Full of Islands—don't marry.
Terminating in a Fork—divorce.
Forked under Mount of Mercury—break of engagement.
Forked at the end—opposite party will break engagement.

VI

CAUTION AGAINST MARRIAGE

If the line is full of islands or downward influence lines, it shows that it is best for the subject not to marry, because his marriage life is not likely to be a happy one.

"Confide in me", the Palmist said;
And then my hand glanced over,
And told me when I was to wed
With my brave soldier lover;

He told me of riches and long life—
Of joy I would discover,
And now I know he told me true—
I've wed my soldier lover.

—Anonymous

Chapter Twenty-Five

THE GOLDEN GIRDLE OF VENUS

Here, indeed, the Girdle of Venus and its mysterious conquering force have done their marvellous task to the everlasting enrichment of human civilization.

—Cheiro

The Girdle of Venus is a symbol of mystic might and Occult knowledge. It gives you telepathy, clairvoyance and titanic strength born of will power that moves mountains and dams the rivers.

I

THE GIRDLE OF VENUS AND RING OF SATURN

Cheiro, the Master Palmist, distinguishes between the Girdle of Venus and the Ring of Saturn as follows:—

"The Girdle of Venus is that broken or unbroken kind of semicircle rising between the first and second fingers and finishing between the third and the fourth."

"The Ring of Saturn is a mark very seldom found, and is not a good sign to have on the hand. I have closely watched the people possessing it, and I have never yet observed that they were in any way successful. It seems to cut off the Mount of Fate in such a peculiar way that such people never gain any point that they may work for or desire."

II

CHARACTER OF THE LINE

Well-Formed

When the Girdle of Venus is well-formed, it shows wit, will, art, literature, occult and mystic powers.

Broken

When the Girdle of Venus is broken, it shows sensuality at its worst.

Cut by Small Lines

When the Girdle of Venus is cut by small lines, it denotes hysteria.

III

ASSOCIATED ATTRIBUTES

Reverses Due to Women

When a Girdle of Venus well-formed is cut by a bar under the Mount of Apollo, it denotes reverses due to women.

Loss of Fortune

A Girdle of Venus in an otherwise bad hand indicates loss of fortune.

Energy and Success

When the Girdle of Venus terminates on the Mount of Mercury, it denotes a great drive and success against all odds.

Spoiled by Passion

Cut near the Mount of Apollo, the Girdle of Venus denotes a life spoiled by a single passion.

Passion For Pleasure

Obstacles to success due to an intense passion for pleasure are denoted when the Girdle of Venus cuts the lines of Liver, Fate and Apollo.

IV

CENTRE OF CONTROVERSY

The Girdle of Venus is a centre of great controversy. Most of the palmists regard it a bad sign.   There are some palmists who think it to be supremely excellent. I include myself in the latter category.

Found in Excellent Hands

Here is Comte C. de Sainte-Germain groping in the darkness in search of light:—

> "But as the Girdle of Venus is also met often in hands otherwise excellent, with the hard palm of the active, practical man or woman, and moderate (if not absent) Mounts of the Moon and Venus, I felt, for years past, that more thorough investigation must be made to complete and correct the meaning ascribed to this line, found so frequently in the hands of some of my most respected American friends; for nowhere else in the world has energy wrought greater miracles and transformed so rapidly into a land of progress and plenty such an immensity of prairies and forests left to waste away since the days of creation. Here, indeed, the Girdle of Venus and its my-

sterious conquering force have done their marvellous task to the everlasting enrichment of human civilization."

Magnetic Influence

Adrian Desbarrolles, French palmist, praises the Girdle of Venus in L. Anneau de Venus:—

"Passions being caused in most cases by a super-abundance of animal, or rather, vital spirits, may be made use of to increase the magnetic influence emanating from these elected creatures whom we feel instinctively to be endowed with genius: it becomes then like a devastating torrent which, between stone-hewn dams, ever kept in the strongest repairs, loses its power for evil and drives instead the wheel of work —and wealth—dispensing factories."

V

ARCH GIFT

"No", said the mysterious strangers;" hadst thou delay-ed the acceptance of the Arch Gift until thou hadst attained to the years, and passed through all the desolate bereavements, that chilled and seared myself, ere my researches had made it mine, thou wouldst have escaped the curse of which thou complainest now, thou wouldst not have mourned over the brevity of human affection as compared to the duration of thine existence; for thou wouldst have survived the very desire and dream of the love of woman. Brigntest, and, but for the error, perhaps the loftiest, of the secret and solemn race that fills up the interval in creation between mankind and the children of the Empyreal, age after age wilt thou rue the

splendid folly which made thee ask to carry the beauty and
the passion of youth into the dreary grandeur of earthly
immortality."

"I do not repent, nor shall I", answered Zanoni. "The
transport and sorrow, so wildly blended, which have at
intervals diversified my doom, are better than the calm
and bloodless tenour of thy solitary way. Thou, who
lovest nothing, hatest nothing, feelest nothing; and walk-
est the world with the noiseless and joyless footstep of
a dream!"

Chapter Twenty-Six

THE TRIANGLE AND QUADRANGLE

God geometrizes.—Plato

The principal lines of the hand divide it into two geometrical figures.

The upper figure is called the Quadrangle.

The lower figure is called the Triangle.

I

THE QUADRANGLE

The Quadrangle is also called the Table of the Hand. As Cheiro says, "The Table of the Hand is the horizontal, elongated square, stretching itself clear across the hand between the Lines of Heart and Head."

Character of the Quadrangle

i. A broad quadrangle denotes broadmindedness.

ii. A narrow quadrangle denotes narrow-mindedness.

iii. Well-formed and large, it shows frankness and outspokenness.

iv. When it is narrow in the centre, it indicates deceitfulness.

Associated Attributes

i. Timidity is indicated by a narrow quadrangle with a drooping Head Line.

ii. Courage is indicated by a broad quadrangle with a
straight Head Line.

Cross and Star

i. A star in the Quadrangle is a token of very great
honour.

ii. A cross in the Quadrangle is an indication of Occult
powers.
A double cross shows very great occult powers.

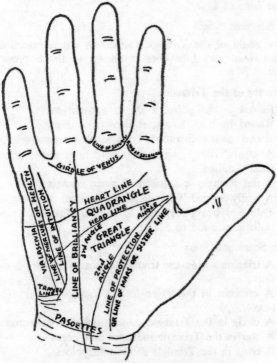

The Triangle and the Quadrangle

II

THE TRIANGLE

The Triangle is also known as the Plain of Mars.

The Plain of Mars is formed by the Line of Life, the Line of Head and the Line of Fate, the Line of Brilliancy or the Line of Liver.

The Supreme Angle

The angle of the Triangle formed by the intersection of the Head and Life lines is known as the Supreme Angle.

Character of the Triangle

i. Raised in the palm, it shows aggressiveness.

ii. Raised in both hands, it depicts courage.

iii. Broad and well-traced Triangle shows generosity.

iv. A clear Triangle with deep pink lines shows good understanding.

v. A flat triangle is a token of mean manners.

vi. A badly-formed Triangle shows avarice.

vii. Pale and heavy Triangle is an indication of materialistic attitude to life.

Bars, Scars and Stars

i. A triangle within the triangle indicates military honours.

ii. A crescent in the Triangle is a symbol of faithfulness.

iii. A circle in the Triangle shows trouble from women.

iv. A star in the Triangle indicates blindness.

v. A cross in the Triangle shows unhappiness.

Chapter Twenty-Seven

SUBORDINATE LINES

These lines have been very interesting to me, as they often revealed peculiar hidden surroundings.

—Martini

I

THE RASCETTE

The Rascette is also called the Bracelets. These are three lines nearest to the palm.

Character of Rascette

i. If the Bracelets are clear and well-defined, they promise health, wealth and happiness.

ii. Poorly formed bracelets indicate a life of extravagance.

Life Expectancy

i. One bracelet clearly marked indicates a life of twenty-three to twenty-eight.

ii. Two unbroken bracelets indicate a life of 46 to 56.

iii. Three unbroken bracelets promise life of 69 to 86.

Associated Attributes

i. Lines from Rascette to the Mount of Moon indicate travel lines.

ii. Lines straight up to the Mount of Mercury indicate wealth suddenly achieved.

iii. Line to the Mount of Apollo indicate success and reputation through big people.

Cross and Angle

i. A cross in the first bracelet indicates a life full of difficulties.
ii. An angle in the bracelets shows money and honour in old age.

II

THE LINE OF MARS

The Line of Mars is the sister line of life. It is also known as the Inner Line of Life.

Character of Mars Line

i. When Mars Line is deep or broad, it shows an irritable spirit.
ii. When the Mars Line is deep and red, it shows a violent passion.

Associated Attributes

i. When it runs close and parallel to Life Line, it mends and repairs all faults and foibles of the Life Line. Its influence is limited to the length it covers along the Life Line.
ii. Mars Line running parallel to Life Line gives a measure of pride to the possessor.

Fork

A fork at the end indicates overflowing animal spirits.

III

LINE OF LIVER

The Line of Liver is also known as the Line of Health. It starts near about the Rascette and goes up towards the Mount of Mercury.

Absence of the Line

This Line of Health is actually a Line of Disease. This is not a Line of Liver but rather a Line of Liver Trouble. Therefore, its absence is a welcome feature. It indicates mental and physical health and financial stability.

Character of Liver Line

i. Long, clear and straight Liver Line indicates good memory.

ii. Irregular and wavy Liver Line indicates poor digestion.

iii. An undulating Liver Line shows biliousness.

iv. Red at the start, Liver Line indicates a bad palpitation of the heart.

v. Thin and red at the centre, it indicates tendency to constant fever.

vi. Yellow Liver Line shows internal complaints.

Associated Attributes

i. Longevity is indicated when it joins Life Line and bracelets are well-formed.

ii. Taking course along the Mount of Moon, it shows many voyages.

iii. Rising to the Mount of Apollo it indicates wealth.

iv. Ascending to the Mount of Mercury it shows a long life.

v. Fainting fits are indicated when it rises from the Life Line.

vi. A heart disease is shown when Liver Line is closely connected with Life Line.

vii. Brain fever is shown when it is entangled with Head Line.

Scars and Stars

i. Dark spot on Liver Line indicates feverish disposition.

ii. A cross shows a very excited imagination.

iii. A triangle on Liver Line shows great occult powers.

iv. A cross high up on the line shows blindness in old age.

v. Many islands indicate weak lungs.

IV

THE LINE OF INTUITION

The Line of Intuition is enclosed within the boundaries of the Mount of Moon. It is also called the Line of Moon.

"In fact it is considered by many authors as a peculiar formation of the Line of Liver or the Via Lasciva, as it is seldom met in a hand that contains either of them."

This line gives an individual an insight into the unknown. It is a very valuable asset. It helps a man to foresee his difficulties and prepare for them long in advance.

Character of Intuition Line

i. Clear and straight, it shows great aptitude for occult powers.

ii. Short and branched, it shows capriciousness.

Associated Attributes

i. Crossed by many small lines, it shows voyages rich in occult values.

ii. When it forms a triangle with Fate Line and Head Line, it gives telepathic powers.

Island

An island at the beginning of Intuition Line indicates somnambulism and clairvoyance.

V

VIA LASCIVA

Via Lasciva is also called the Milky Way. It runs close along the palm, at the edge, opposite the Line of Life, and usually acts as a sister line of the Line of Liver.

Character of Milky Way

i. Traced vividly in both hands, it shows sensuality.

ii. Starting from inside the Mount of Venus, it indicates lasciviousness.

Associated Attributes

i. It shows great happiness and excellent health when Milky Way acts as a sister line of Liver Line.

ii. Good luck, eloquence and talent as a statesman is indicated when it reaches up to the Mount of Mercury.

iii. It indicates health when joined to the Mount of Apollo by an Influence Line.

VI

FINGER LINES

The first phalanx is nailed.
The second phalanx is in the middle.
The third phalanx is close to the palm.

Star

A star on the second phalanx shows habitual cheerfulness.

Sudden Death

One short vertical line traced on all the joints indicates sudden death.

Horizontal Lines

Horizontal lines on first phalanx indicate bad health.

Literary Success

Indicated by a cross on the upper joint of the first finger.

Occult Powers

Occult powers are indicated by a triangle.

Waving Vertical Lines

indicate fatal happenings.

Great Fame

Great fame is indicated by a line running along the length of the entire finger.

Scientific Pursuits

A line on the first phalanx shows success in scientific pursuits.

Two Stars

Two stars on third phalanx indicate dishonourable death.

VII

THE CHILDREN LINES

The Children Lines are indicated at the base of the little finger, near the Marriage Line.

i. Deeply marked lines—male children.
ii. Faintly marked lines—female children.
iii. Straight lines—healthy children.
iv. Wavy lines—weak children.

These children's lines are more reliable on mother's hand than on father's hand.

VIII

TRAVEL LINES

The travel lines ar found on the edge of the palm on the lower part of the hand.

Cross
A cross on the Journey Line indicates disappointment.

Square
shows protection from harm on a journey.

Broken
A broken line shows an unpleasant trip.

Two Travel Lines
Indicate repetition of the trip.

Touching Life Line

When a Travel Line touches Life Line, it shows death on a journey.

IX

SIGNIFICANCE OF STAR

"The star", says Cheiro, "is a sign of very great importance, whenever it makes its appearance on the hand. I do not at all hold that it is generally a bad sign, a danger, and one from which there is no escape; rather, on the contrary, I consider it, with one or two exceptions, a fortunate sign, and one which should generally depend upon the portion of the hand on the line with which it is connected."

Chapter Twenty-Eight

DETERMINATION OF DATES

Time is not an item on the map. Past, Present and Future
are not depicted on any automobile map, although they would
necessarily be present on any trip. This map is an over-all
view merging time and distance. Similarly, if the panorama
of one's life were imprinted on some level of the mind, one
might call it a fourth-dimensional survey of one's entire life
and experience. But that part of the mind which is without
natural limitations must be vividly aware too, that the personal
journey is but the minutest fragment of a line inextricably
blended into a map immense enough to contain all the bil-
lions of contemporaneous journeys. What a mysterious map
indeed, charting the way for the great march of humanity
towards the undisclosed destination!

—Rita Van Alen

Palmistry is a map of the Great Unknown Country.
Its pioneers are the great sagacious and studious palmists.
Every great palmistry charts new territory and brings it
within the knowledge of all. This conquest of the occult
knowledge has been going on for hundreds of years. Thus
Comte C.De Sainte-Germaine declares:—

"Remember, once for all, the Palmistry is not the
system of one man, and that no one man's existence
is long enough to create the hundreth part of a new
system—if such an undertaking were possible or desirable."

The years are marked both on the Line of Life and
the Line of Fate. All mounts are connected with them

by means of influence rays. All the events of life can
be dated according to different methods chalked out by
different palmists on the basis of experience.

I

GOLDEN GUIDANCE

Right and Left

Both the hands should be used for the proper assessment of dates and other things, even though there are
differences between the two, as Josef Ronald points out:—

"The pattern of lines in one hand appears like
mirror image of the other. There is however some
noticeable difference that is significant, as, for instance, in the shape and appearance of the corresponding lines of the hands. The relation of the left
to the right hand is that of promise and fulfilment
of the architect's plan and the builder's accomplishment.

Difference and Divergence

There is a different divergence in hands due to shape
and general size of the body. This must be kept in view
while evaluating dates:—

"A hand with a long slender palm will have the
figures on the lines thrown much farther apart than
will be the case in a short broad hand. But experience will quickly allow the student to make proper
allowance for these differences and give him the sure
look that will divide the Lines of Life and Fate into
properly sized sections without any other compasses
than the pair we possess in our eyes."

II

CHEIRO'S METHOD

Cheiro advocates a System of Seven. Measure the Life Line or Fate Line with a thread. Divide the thread into seven equal parts. Each part will denote thirteen years so that seven parts will denote ninty-one years.

Cheiro explains why he follows the System of Seven as follows:—

> "In the first place, we find from a medical and scientific standpoint the seven as the most important point of calculation. We find that the entire system undergoes a complete change every seven years; that the brain takes seven forms before it takes upon itself the unique character of the human brain, and so forth. Again, we find that in all ages the number seven has played a most important part in the history of the world, as, for instance, the seven races of humanity, the seven gods of the seven planets, the seven days of the week, the seven colours, the seven minerals, the supposition of the seven senses, the three parts of the body each containing seven sections, and the seven divisions of the world. Again in the Bible seven is the most important number; but it is superflous to give further details."

Another Cheiro Method

i. Where the Fate Line cuts the Head Line, it denotes thirty-five years.

ii. The Fate Line cuts the Heart Line at fifty-six.

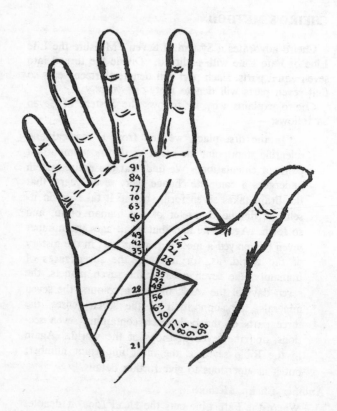

Cheiro's Method

III

JENNINGS' METHOD

Alice Denton Jennings suggests the following method:—

"For the purpose of reading age on the lines, it is assumed that the average human life (excepting in rare cases) does not greatly exceed seventy years.

"Time is counted downward on the Life Line, beginning at the starting of the line under the index finger and ending at the wrist. For convenience and to facilitate quickness in reading, divide the line in the centre, fixing that point at the age of 36 which is approximately one half on seventy. Proportion the space above and the space below as representing different ages of the life.

"Time is counted across the hand on the Heart Line. The beginning point for measuring is under the index-finger, regardless of where the line itself starts. Divide the line in the centre, fixing the point as 36. Proportion the space before and after, following the same rule as given for estimating time on the Life Line.

"Time is counted upward on the Fate Line, starting from the wrist and going towards the Mount of Saturn. Divide the line in the centre, fixing the point as 36. Proportion the space before and after, following the same rule as given for estimating time on the Life Line."

NATURAL DIVISION

36th Year
Where the Fate Line joins the Head Line.
56th Year
Where Fate Line joins the Heart Line.
70th Year
Where the Fate Line reaches the root of the second finger.

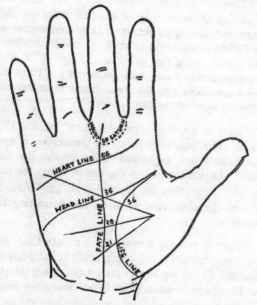

Natural Division

Chapter Twenty-Nine

SCIENTIFIC APPROACH TO PALMISTRY

Mankind are earthen jugs with spirits in them.

—Hawthorne

Palmistry is the science of tendencies rather than prophecies. It deals with things and events that may happen, not that they must happen.

Happenings foretold by Palmistry happen under certain conditions. When these conditions are not there, these do not happen. These conditions are not unchangeable. These can be altered with more or less effort. And when these conditions are changed, these events do not happen.

Palmistry tells you what good things you can expect from the present course of your career; and how those things can be brightened up. It also tells you what evils are in your way; and how you can bypass them by changing your course of career.

There is no fatal inevitability about the predictions of Palmistry, and no inevitable fatality. Everything alters when it alteration finds. Therefore your good qualities need not puff you, because the very pride of them will reduce their value; nor should your faults and foibles depress you because these are all changeable.

I

NO HASTY HIGHWAY, NO ROSY RUNWAY

Palmistry is no hasty highway, no rosy runway. You cannot see hands of people at a bus stand while waiting for your conveyance. You must take time over each hand to assess its sweetness and strength, vice and wickedness.

The best way is to take impressions and study them at leisure. For impressions of the hand use printer's ink, especially that used by the police for taking fingerprints of the criminals. The ink is available from any stationery store. It is good to use glazed paper for the purpose. A few drops of petrol will remove the ink from the hands.

A matter of Combination

You must study the hand from all angles—mounts, lines, thumb, fingers, nails, etc.—before risking your final judgment. As William G. Benham says, "The success of hand-reading is a matter of combination. The type of the subject must be combined with his energy, brain power, good intentions, vices, health conditions, and other important factors before a balance can be struck."

II

STUDY OF THE WHORLS

While studying the lines, do not forget the whorls. Every hand has some mysterious fingerprint whorls. These have been described by Mrs. Nelie Simmons Meier in her book **The Lion Paws.** These whorls are formed by capillaries in the skin pigment. "If you have any whorls in your hand", says Rita Van Alen, "you are to be considered fortunate indeed."

i. A whorl under the first finger, on the Mount of Jupiter, gives intuitive powers.

ii. A whorl under the second finger gives wisdom and vision to avoid any serious pitfalls in life.

iii. Under the third finger a whorl gives Sixth Sense, occult powers, occult wisdom, telepathy and clairvoyance.

iv. Between third and fourth finger, a whorl gives artistic powers and the capability to commercialize art.

III

RING OF SOLOMON

The Ring of Solomon is a branch of the Line of Heart encircling the Mount of Saturn. It gives great powers of occult, intuition and clairvoyance. One having this Ring of Solomon knows much more about himself than a palmist can tell him. Be his student rather than his teacher. Try to learn from the secret of the lines on his hand. Without being a palmist he knows more about palmistry than an expert and experienced Professor of Palmistry.

Sex Differences

A true student of palmistry should not be bothered about artificial sex differences. There may be more of man in a woman and more of woman in a man than you can judge superficially. Palmistry will give you right guidance if you are not prejudiced against it. Thus Alexander Dumas has it:—

"If you pass to the general signs, I tell you that, although a woman, you have a soldier's hand, combative and imperious. You like bodily exercise, movement, horses. You have very fine tact. None of your sentiments proceed from reason; but on the contrary, you act instinctively, by sympathy or antipathy. Had you been a man, you would have been a soldier; free to follow your own calling, you would have been an actress."

IV

EMANATION FROM HEAVENLY BODIES

Man is not earth, earthy. Do not try to take too much materialistic look of things. Follow the spiritual instinct,

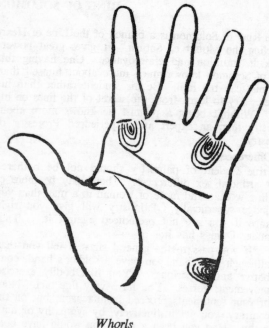

Whorls

because Palmistry is essentially an occult science. As Comte C.de Sainte-Germain declares, "This science proclaims that the astral fluid is an emanation from the principal heavenly bodies that surround the earth. That this emanation returns whence it came and is again emitted in a kind of perspiration."

Suicidal Tendencies

These are emanations from heavenly bodies that produce suicidal tendencies in persons and these should be carefully noticed and noted. These are the features of a possible suicide case:—

> "The hand is generally long, with a sloping Line of Head, and a developed Mount of Luna, particularly towards the base. The Line of the Head is also very much connected with the Line of Life, and so increases the sensitive nature of the subject. In such a case the individual would not naturally be morbid or even show the inclination for suicide, but so imaginative that any trouble, grief or scandal is intensified a thousandfold, and to kill or injure self gives the peculiar satisfaction of self-martyrdom to such a type."

V

A COSMIC STUDY

Palmistry is a cosmic study. Through a man we study the universe. Through universe we study the man. Palmistry is not merely in the hand of the man. The entire

human knowledge can lead us in that direction. Thus
Rita Van Alen declares:—

"Like other people my early attention to the significance of the hands came as a result of my interest
in music. To think that the hand was all important in bringing to life all the beauty, colour and
harmony of sounds, profoundly interested me."

The Hand Speaks Out

The hand speaks louder than the tongue if you have
eyes to see and ears to hear. Thus Balzac lays down:—

"We acquire the faculty of imposing silence upon
our lips, upon our eyes, upon our eyebrows, and upon
our foreheads; the hand alone does not dissemble
. . . no feature is more expressive than the hand."

As Aristotle declared, "The hand is the organ of
organs, the active agent of the passive powers of the
entire system."

VI

THUMB AND HEAD

As I wrote·in another book, "There is an intimate connection between the head and the thumb of a person.
There is a thumb in the head. There is a head in the
thumb. There is no high road to the head of a man. The
way that goes up to the head of a person is a narrow
path. It is a path as narrow as the thumb of a man."

Nothing Is Impossible

As Balzac lays down, "When one thinks that the line
separating our flesh from the growing nail contains the

unexplainable and inexplicable and invisible mystery of the incessant transformation of our fluid into horn, one must admit that nothing is impossible in the marvellous transformation of human constituting elements.

A Perfect Machine

"There has never been conceived or made by man any instrument", says William C. Benham, "machine or contrivance, capable of such a diversity of usefulness as the human hand. Nothing has ever existed with such infinite adaptability to various needs or capable of being trained to such degrees of dexterity or versatility. Nor is it likely that as perfect a machine will ever be produced by human skill, for the only thing that the human hand cannot do is to create an instrument as perfect as itself."

Chapter Thirty

HOW TO DETERMINE YOUR CAREER

It has been the endeavour of all those whom the world has reverenced for superior wisdom, to persuade man to be acquainted with himself, to learn his own powers and his own weaknesses, to observe by what evils he is most dangerously be set, and by what temptations most easily overcome.

—Samuel Johnson

Work is worship. Your job in life is your religion. Happy is the man who has found his religion. Happier still is the man who has found his job. Your religion is meaningless if it is not a part of your work. Your work is senseless if it is not a part of your work.

Most of the people are unhappy today because they are like square pegs in round holes. They love not the work they do. Overcome by opportunism they have taken jobs and appointments in which they have no heart. Having no heart in your work is to be disloyal to your employer and false to yourself. In the long run these people harm themselves much more than they injure their employers. Their life is discontented and these disjointed people are in majority everywhere in the world. Consequently, despite all the advantages offered by a scientific civilization, most of the people are mentally, morally and materially very miserable. Like Mephistopheles they are serving the devil for food, clothes, houses, radios, refrigerators and motor cars.

"Lead me not into temptation", said Jesus Christ. These people have willingly and voluntarily walked into the spider's web of temptuous temptations. They have no feet. They know not where they are. They lack bearing of their occupation, because they have no interest in it. They have bowed to the Satan for a temporary relief. The permanent tranquillity which comes out of doing in what one is really interested is denied to them. Better a beggar who loves his fiddle than a king who feels on the throne. Everybody admires the British King, Edward VIII, who renounced his kingdom for Mrs. Simpson. As Duke of Windsor he still enjoys the life he loves and he has never regretted the relinquishment of his right to the British throne. On the contrary, his younger brother, George VI, who stepped into his shoes, is long dead and buried, weighed down by the weight of British monarchy for which he was not bred and brought up and which fell on him like a bolt from the blue.

George VI was not destined to be the British King, and he should not have lured himself into accepting the tempting offer of kingship. Little wonder, he paid the price for it with his early death. That is happening all round us. People live fast and they die fast. They suffer from neurosis and nervous breakdown and lunacy. The hospitals are full of these modern maniacs. Despite the scientific conquest of the modern diseases, the number of doctors and drugs is multiplying by leaps and bounds. Today more people die of drugs than of diseases. That is the price we pay for not living in harmony with nature.

I

SCIENCE OF HARMONY

Palmistry is the Science of Harmony. It teaches you how to live in harmony with Mother Nature. It does not tell you to break the laws of nature. It only tell you what stumbling blocks in your way are and how these

can be removed according to laws of nature. Thirst, for
example, is natural; but to drink water to quench it is
equally natural. If instead of water one tries to quench
his thirst by drinking kerosene oil, one is bound to destroy himself without quenching his thirst. That is exactly
what most of us are doing today. We are eating arsenic
to satisfy our hunger. Not knowing the right course to
remove hurdles from our path, we fight the windmills
blindfold like Don Quixote and then blame our destiny
for having let us down.

This is what Jean Nicot says to Viola in Zanoni:—

> "Actress, you must hear me! If you know what
> this calling of the stage is in the eyes of prejudice—
> that is, of the common opinion of mankind. It is
> to be a Princess before the lamps, and a Pariah before
> the day. No man believes in your virtue, no man
> credits your vows; you are the puppet that they
> consent to trick out with tinsel for their amusement,
> not an idol for their worship. Are you so enamoured
> of this career that you scorn even to think of secu-
> rity and honour? Perhaps you laugh at the prejudice
> that would degrade you, and would wisely turn it
> to advantage."

So an actress should be fully aware of his destiny and
should not merely live in a fool's paradise. The stage
career does not usually have a happy termination. Quite
a few actresses commit suicide. The most recent example
is that of Marilyn Monroe, the most successful Hollywood
actress. She committed suicide, because having all, she
felt she had nothing. She rolled in millions and had every
creature comfort, and yet nothing but futility and frustration suffocated her to death. On the contrary, Greta
Garbo even in her old age still commands the millions
to worship her. Why? For Marilyn Monroe it was a
piecework for wages. For Greta Garbo it is a religion.
So it was for Henry Ford. William C. Richards writes
about the latter:—

"He considered a full day's work holy and he had exhaustless zeal. Attacked on every side save that of his private life, no scandal brushed Fair Lane. He did not believe in set hours of work but thought a worker ought to work as long as he was able; and should enjoy his work so much that he would almost count the time lost when he was not working . . . .

"The young man between eighteen and twenty-one has to show himself sober and saving, and satisfy the company that the money paid him would not 'be frittered on high living. 'Riotous' was the word used.

"A married man had to live with and take care of his family, and single men over twenty-two were to be thrifty, likewise. A rule was sought by which all men could live comfortably and Ford arrogated to himself the right to impose on others the one he lived by as a rather nice model. Since employment by the company under the new arrangement would be pecuniarily desirable, he used profit-sharing as a lever by which to descipline rowdies who did not behave the way he thought they should."

Had Henry Ford been a palmist, he could have used better methods to guide the young men in his factories towards their bright careers. But these are now within your reach.

II

POINTS TO NOTE

Take an impression of your hand with printer's ink or just make a rough drawing so that you can have a record and you can find later in life what changes of lines have occurred in your hands in the course of your career due to certain changes in your habits, thoughts and activities.

Take a notebook and go on jotting therein all the points mentioned in this book, so far as they are concerned with the indications mapped out on your hand. Go from chapter to chapter, noting everything that concerns you.

Empty Hand or Full Hand?

See if your hand is empty or full, as mentioned in Chapter One. Empty hand means that you have only a few clearcut lines. A full hand means that it is fraught with criss-cross lines. The more line you have in your hand, the more confused will be your mind. A man with a confused mind should not try to walk the road of life independently. He should find an adviser whom he can trust.

Size of the Hand

See whether you have short, large or medium hands, as described in Chapter Four. People with large hands have a passion for details. People with small hands are only interested in the blueprints of big projects. Only a person with large hands will be able to make a success of a small concern with small finance. A person with small hands and small finance should rather seek employment so that he lacks the opportunity to fritter away his own funds in wild-goose pursuits.

Other points in Chapter Four should also be noted so far as these concern your hands.

The Type of Hand

Turn to Chapter Five and note down whether your hand is Elementary, Square, Spatulate, Angular, etc. Note the important characteristics of your hand on the basis of this classification in your notebook.

Fingers Thumb and Nails

Note down the characteristics of your fingers, thumb and nails as mentioned in chapter Seven to Ten. Here you will have a gold-mine of knowledge about your character and career.

The Type of Man You Are

Study chapters Eleven to Fifteen, find out your Mounts and to what type you belong—Jupiterian, Saturnian, Apolloian, Mercurian, etc. This can provide you another treasure of useful knowledge about your inner self.

As Rita Van Alen says, "One of the best combinations for a successful business man is the hand with both Jupiterian and Mercurian Mount developments. Here we have the ambition of the Jupiterian backed by the shrewdness of the Mercurian."

Lines of Career and Character

Study Chapters Seventeen to Twenty-Seven and note down all major indications concerning your hands.

III

BALANCE SHEET

With all the indications listed in your notebook draw up a balance sheet of your assets and liabilities—virtues and vices, points of strength and weakness.

On one side you write qualities as mentioned in the book on the basis of indications in your hand. On the other side you write your shortcomings, faults and foibles.

Then evaluate your assets and liabilities. Sometimes a single fault may be equal to ten virtues. Sometimes a single virtue may be equal to a hundred faults. For example, if you have a square hand, a small Fate Line means much. On the contrary, on a Spatulate hand, even a long Fate Line may not be very helpful.

Having known your defects and qualities, drawn up a mental picture of yourself not as a messy man but as a mathematical machine. In the background of your vices and virtues see what you can do and what you cannot do. What you can do the best in the totality of existing conditions is your Career.

IV

SECRETS OF NATURE

You can avoid the pitfalls and overcome your faults and foibles by observing the indications in your hand. For every malady there is also a remedy. When you have observed an evil sign in your hand, you willl be able to overcome by following up some strong point in your hand to overcome that. For example, if there is a break in your Life Line, find out the approximate years, according to the method mentioned in Chapter Twenty-Eight. In those years take a very great care of your health and do not take any kind of risk. For example, avoid travelling by air or rash driving or taking heavy doses of liquor and all kinds of unhygienic foodstuffs. There is every reason for you to survive despite the warning of death on your hand. There is no inevitability about Palmistry. It is only a science of probabilities.

"The ides are come, not gone."

"Tush! If he be the soothsayer, you are not the Caesar. It is your vanity that makes you credulous.

Thank Heaven, I do not think myself of such importance, that the operations of nature should be changed in order to frighten me."

"But why should the operations of nature be changed? There may be a deeper philosophy than we dream of—a philosophy that discovers the secrets of nature, but does not alter, by penetrating, its courses."

Chapter Thirty-One

CAREERS FOR STUDENTS

When, then, the pupil is thus initiated and prepared, let him open the casement, light the lamps, and bathe his temples with elixir. He must beware how he presume yet to quaff the volatile and fiery spirit. To taste, till repeated inhalations have accustomed the frame gradually to the ecstatic liquid, is to know not life, but death.

—The Secret Book of Mejnour in Zanoni.

One should work up to his career slowly and steadily by golden but gradual steps directed one who has your weal and welfare nearest and dearest to his head and heart. A sudden jump to a great golden gallop of a career activated by shamefaced opportunism and get-rich-quick ambition can only lead you to live-fast-and-die-early span of life.

Oh "yes", forsooth, Clarence Glyndon! Every light nature answers "yes" lightly to such a question from lips so rosy! Have a care—have a care! Why the deuce, Mejnour, do you leave your pupil of four-and-twenty to the mercy of these cats-a-mountain! Preach fast, abstinence sublime renunciation of the cheats of the senses! Very well in you, sir, heaven knows how many ages old! But, at four-and-twenty, your Hierophant, would have kept out of Fillide's way, or you would have had small taste for the cabals!

And so they stood, and talked and vowed, and whispered, till the girl's mother made some noise within the house, and Fillide bounded back to the distaff, her finger once more on her lip.

"There is more magic in Fillide than in Mejnour", said Glyndon to himself, walking gaily home; "yet on second thoughts, I know not if I quite so well like a character so ready for revenge! But he who has the real secret can baffle even the vengeance of a woman, and disarm all danger!"

Sirrah! dost thou even already meditate the possibility of treason? Oh, well said Zanoni, "to pour pure water into the muddy well does but disturb the mud!"

I

AN ACTOR'S HAND

Do you want to be an actor? Every student wants to be an actor, but few of them—very few of them—indeed succeed. And "success" itself is a very dubious word. Do you want to be an actor? Or do you want to make money by working as an actor in the films? The two questions are quite different. If it were merely a desire for acting, anybody can be a actor. In fact, everybody is an actor. Prime Minister Nehru declared long before he achieved that position that his success in public life is due to the fact that he has the art of "showmanship". In more candid terms, he is an actor!

Everybody in the modern world is an actor, because without acting any measure of social success is an impossibility. But if you want to act on the stage and make money and find fame, it is a different thing. Above everything else you need a strong Fate Line. If fate is not on your side how do other qualities help you? You may be a very good actor and yet die a pauper. To be a business man is one thing but make money in business is quite another. And acting too is a kind of business in the actor, his movements, his gestures and emotions are his capital.

If you have a strong Fate Line which goes straight up to the Mount of Apollo, you have very high chances of being success in the film world; and if the Mount of Apollo is well-developed, your social popularity is assured. If the Fate Line runs up to the Mount of Jupiter, your showmanship may make you a great politician, a great leader, a minister; and if it goes up to the Mount of Mercury, you will make great money out of your acting in business or the business of acting, even though your qualities as an actor may be far inferior to those of others.

You also need a long Line of Head which should preferably be forked at the termination. A short Line of Head will not give you a comprehensive understanding of human feelings which an actor should have.

A good actor usually has a palm shorter than the fingers which have conical tips; and the fourth finger is very good. But these things are not indispensable indications. A strong thumb showing will-power can override many obstacles which otherwise pest and pester the thorny road to this ivory tower in a rose garden.

If the Mount of Mercury is strong, it is an additional support to making money out of the actor's profession, even though it is not of a very high order. Not all great actors are rich. The truth is those who act poorly live richly; and those who are rich in their artistic qualities die with empty pockets.

And remember that nobody can be a great actor without training and encouragement. Acting does not come naturally to a person like writing poetry. Even writing poetry is not so natural as many people think. Poets spend long vigils over single lines. Everything comes with training. The lines on your hand are helpful only when the necessary training and technique is there. With determination and proper training you can be a great actor

even if all the lines on your hand run contrary to the
hand of a standard actor. Palmistry is not a science of
fatality. It gives you a ticket for Hollywood but cannot
force you to go there. That is your own choice. But
training is easy when the lines are perfect or necessary
will is there. This is how Viola became a great actor
but as the daughter of a great musician of Naples she
had the inherent qualities in her, because you cannot
light a matchstick without inflammatory material, however hard you strike it against the matchbox. You can
only break the match stick without producing any fire
or light:—

All this helped silently to weave charmed webs
over Viola's imagination, that afterthought and later
years might labour vainly to dispel. And all this
especially fitted her to hang, with a fearful joy, upon
her father's music. Those visionary strains, ever
struggling to translate into wild and broken sounds
the language of unearthly beings, breathed around
her from her birth.

Thus you might have said that her whole mind
was full of music—associations, memories, sensations
of pleasure or pain, all were mixed up inexplicably
with those sounds that now delighted, and now terri-
fied—that greeted her when her eyes opened to the
sun, and woke her trembling on her lonely couch
in the darkness of the night.

The legends and tales of Gionetta only served to
make the child better understand the signification
of those mysterious tones; they furnished her with
words to the music. It was natural that the daughter
of such a parent should soon evince some taste in
his art. But this developed chiefly in the ear and
the voice. She was yet a child when she sang divinely.

A great Cardinal—great alike in the State and
the Conservatorio, heard of her gifts and sent for
her. From that moment her fate was decided; she

was to be the future glory of Naples, the prima donna of San Carlo. The Cardinal insisted upon the accomplishment of his own predictions, and provided her with the most renowned masters. To inspire her with emulation, his Eminence took her one evening to his own box: it would be something to see the performance, something more to hear the applause lavished upon the glittering signoras she was hereafter to excel!

Oh, how gloriously the Life of the Stage—that fairy world of Music and Song, dawned upon her! It was the only world that seemed to correspond with her strange childish thoughts. It appeared to her as if, cast hitherto on a foreign shore, she was brought at last to see the forms and hear the language of her native land.

Beautiful and true enthusiasm, rich with the promise of genius! Boy or man, thou will never be a poet, if thou hast not felt the ideal, the romance, the Calypso's isle that opened to thee, when for the first time, the magic curtain was drawn aside, and let in the World of Poetry on the World of Prose!

And now the initiation was begun. She was to read, to study, to depict by a gesture, a look, the passion she was to delineate on the boards; lessons dangerous, in truth, to some but not to the pure enthusiasm that comes from Art; for the mind that rightly conceives Art, is but a mirror, which gives back what is cast on its surface only—while unsullied. She seized on nature and truth intuitively. Her recitations became full of unconscious power; her voice moved the heart to tears, or warmed it into generous rage. But this rose from that sympathy which genius ever has, even in its earliest innocence, with whatever feels, or aspires or suffers. It was no premature woman comprehending the love or jealousy that the words expressed; her art was one of those strange secrets which the psychologists may unriddle to us if they please, and tell us why children of the simplest minds and the purest hearts are often so acute to distinguish, in the tales you tell them, or the songs you sing, the difference between the true Art and the False—Passion and Jargon—Homer and Racine; echoing back, from hearts that have not yet felt what they repeat, the melodious accents of the natural pathos.

So this is what makes a great actor—lines or no lines on the hand! Mere daydreaming, on a back bench in the classroom, of Raj Kapoor, Nargis and others will not make you an actor. Be warned in time: You have got to work for it.

II

ADMINISTRATIVE ABILITY

If you want to join the I.A.S., I.F.S., I.A.A.S. or other top services, look for the Triangle of Administrative Ability in the centre of the palm, below the middle finger. If you have this triangle, it is sufficient by itself to assure you a big administrative post, not necessarily through a competitive examination. You can get it direct through Union Public Service Commission or on contract from the government—owned business undertakings. Some European business concerns, like the Burmah Shell, Lever Brothers and Esso, offer even better and more remunerative administrative posts than the Government of India.

Success through a competitive examination, as such, is not indicated in the main lines on the palm; but one with a long line of head, a strong aggressive thumb, and the Mounts of Mars and Mercury, is ready to fight for material advantages. And that indicates success in any competitive examination.

A student aspiring to make his mark in a competitive examination should have some of the following marks:—

   i. A long and straight line of Head.

   ii. The Line of Head and Life should not be joined at the start, but there should be a short gap between the two.

   iii. A vivid, deep Line of Life without breaks.

   iv. A long Fate Line going up to the Mount of Jupiter or Apollo.

   v. A cross between the lines of Head and Heart.

   vi. No downward lines of influence on the Line of Life, Head and Heart.

   vii. Line of Apollo.

   viii. Mount of Jupiter, Apollo or Mercury well-developed.

   ix. A good strong thumb.

   x. A square or spatulate hand.

   xi. Clear rosy well-shaped nails.

   xii. No Line of Health or Milky Way.

   xiii. No Girdle of Venus.

   xiv. Fate Line not entangled with Life Line near the wrist.

   xv. Fate Line should start from the wrist and go straight up.

It should be remembered that from the signs of the hand there will not be much difference between the ministerial post and that of a gazetted officer. A secretary often commands more power and dignity than the minister. The signs on the hand show authority and not the label on the chair that you occupy. You may not be a king but a king-maker or a minister who holds the king under his thumb.

The difference between a minister and a secretary is that between a royal guest and a robber who guards the royal guest:—

Glydon's heart somewhat failed him as he looked around, and the question he desired to ask died upon his lips. At length, from one of the dismal cabins emerged a form superior to the rest. Instead of the patched and ragged overall, which made the only garment of the men he had hitherto seen, the dress of this person was characterized by all the trappings of the national bravery. Upon his raven hair, the glossy curls of which made a notable contrast to the matted and elfin locks of the savages around was placed a cloth cap with a gold tassel that hung down to his shoulder, his mustaches were trimmed with care, and a silk kerchief of gay colours was twisted round a well-shaped but sinewy throat; a short jacket of rough cloth was decorated with several rows of gilt filgree buttons; his nether garments fitted tight to his limbs, and were curiously braided; while, in a broad parti-coloured sash, were placed two silver-hilted pistols, and the sheathed knife, usually worn by Italians of the lower order, mounted in ivory elaborately carved. A small carbine of handsome workmanship was slung across his shoulder, and completed his costume. The man himself was of middle-size, athletic yet slender, with straight and regular features, sun-burnt but not swarthy; and an expression of countenance which, though reckless and bold, had in it frankness rather than ferocity, and, if defying, was not altogether unprepossessing.

Glydon, after eyeing this figure for some moments with great attention, checked his rein, and asked the way to the "Castle of the Mountain."

The man lifted his cap as he heard the question, and, approaching Glyndon, laid his hand upon the neck of the horse, and said, in a low voice, "Then you are the cavalier whom our patron the signor expected. He bade me wait for you here, and lead you to the castle. And indeed, signor, it might have been unfortunate if I had neglected to obey the command."

The man then, drawing a little aside, called out to the bystanders, in a loud voice, "Ho, ho! my friends, pay henceforth and forever all respect to this worshipful cavalier. He is the expected guest of our blessed patron of the Castle of the Mountain. Long life to him! May he, like his host, be safe by day and by night—on the hill and in the waste—dagger and the bullet—in limb and in life! Cursed against the dagger and the bullet—in limb and in life! Cursed be he who touches a hair of his head, or a baiocho in his pouch. Now and for ever we will protect and honour him—for the law or against the law—with the faith and to the death. Amen! Amen!"

"Amen!" responded, in wild chorus, a hundred voices; and the scattered and straggling groups pressed up the street, nearer and nearer to the horseman.

"And that he may be known", continued the Englishman's strange protector, "to the eye and to the ear, I place around him the white sash and I give him the sacred watchword—'Peace to the Brave'. Signor, when you wear this sash, the proudest in these parts will bare the head and bend the knee. Signor, when you utter this watchword, the bravest hearts will be bound to your bidding. Desire you safety, or ask you revenge—to again a beauty or lose a foe—speak but the word, and we are yours— we are yours! Is it not so, comrades?" And again the hoarse voice shouted, "Amen, Amen!"

"Now, signor," whispered the bravo, "if you have a few coins to spare, scatter them amongst the crowd, and let us be gone."

Glyndon, not displeased at the concluding sentence, emptied his purse in the streets; and while, with mingled oaths, blessings, shrieks, and yells, men, women, and children scrambled for the money, the bravo, taking the rein of the horse, led it a few paces through the village at a brisk trot, and then, turning up a narrow lane to the left, in a few minutes neither houses nor men were visible, and the mountains closed their path on either side. It was then that, releasing his bridle and slackening his pace, the guide turned his dark eyes on Glyndon with an arch expression, and said—.

"Your Excellency was not perhaps prepared for the hearty welcome we have given you."

"Why in truth, I ought to have been prepared for it, since the signor to whose house I am bound, did not disguise from me the character of the neighbourhood."

This is how the Secretaries dramatize the might and magnificence of the Ministers in the "Castle of the Mountain" called the Government of India. The lines for both being similar, it does not matter whether you become a minister or a minister's man, a Valmiki or a highwayman. With the lines of power and authority on your hand, you taste power in some way or the other. And who does not know as a secretary you have the last laugh at the minister?

III

ARCHITECTURAL ENGINEER

If you are planning to become an Architectural Engineer, your hand will show the following signs:—

    i.   A straight Line of Head.
   ii.   A long finger of Saturn.
  iii.   The first phalanx of fingers long.
  iv.   Long straight spatulate Finger of Apollo.
   v.   Strong Mount of Venus.
  vi.   Mount of Apollo excellent.
 vii.   Mount of Mercury good.
viii.   Long second phalanx of thumb.
  ix.   Long square nails.

It is not necessary that you should have all the indications. As many as half of them qualify you for the career. The rest depends upon your determination and training.

It needs not merely the technical skill but idealism to be a great Architectural Engineer like those who built our ancient temples, Taj Mahal and Chandigarh. You are not building for merely men of today but for the coming generations. Such houses, as Christ said, should be built upon the rock and like the rock:—'The flower gives perfume to the rock on whose bosom it grows. A little while, and the flower is dead; but the rock still endures;—the snow at its breast—the sunshine on its summit."

IV

AN ARTIST'S HAND

The hand of a great artist has the following indications:—

    i.   The Line of Apollo starting from the Line of Life.

ii. An influence line from the Line of Head rising up to the Mount of Apollo.

iii. Line of Fate terminating on the Mount of Apollo.

iv. Good Mount of Luna.

v. Good space between the fingers of Jupiter and Saturn.

vi. A pointed finger of Jupiter.

vii. Large first phalanx of the Finger of Apollo.

viii. A good straight long finger of Apollo.

But lines alone do not make an artist. One has to live art and make it the breath of one's being in order to become a great artist. These are significant passages from Bulwer Lytton's **Zanoni**:—

> As some injudicious master lowers and vitiates the taste of the student by fixing his attention to what he falsely calls the Natural, but which, in reality, is the Commonplace and understands not the beauty in art is created by what Raffaele so well describes— viz. **the idea of beauty in the painter's own mind:** and that in every art, whether its plastic expression be found in words or marble, colours or sounds, the servile imitation of nature is the work of the journey-men and tyros;—so in conduct the man of the world vitiates and lowers the bold enthusiasm of loftier natures by the perpetual reduction of whatever is generous and trustful to all that is trite and coarse. A great German poet has well defined the distinction between discretion and the larger wisdom. In the last there is a certain rashness which the first dis-dains—.
>
> "The purblind see but the receding shore.
> Not that to which the bold wave wafts them o'er."
>
> Yet in this logic of the prudent and the wordly there is often a reasoning unanswerable of its kind.

You must have a feeling—a faith in whatever is self-sacrificing and divine—whether in religion or in art, in glory or in love—or Commonsense will reason you out of the sacrifice, and a syllogism will debase The Divine to an article in the market.

Every true critic in art, from Aristotle and Pliny —from Winkelman and Vassari, to Reynolds and Fuseli, has sought to instruct the painter that Nature is not to be copied, but **exalted**: that the loftiest order of art, selecting only the loftiest combinations, is the perpetual struggle of humanity to approach the Gods. The great painter, as the great author, embodies what is **possible to man,** it is true, but what is not **common to mankind.** There is truth in Hamlet; in Macbeth, and his witches, in Desdemona; in Othello, in Prospero; and in Caliban; there is truth in the cartoons of Raffaele; there is truth in the Apollo, the Antinoiis, and the Laocoon. But you do not meet the originals of the words, the cartoons, or the marble, in Oxford-street or St. James's. All these, to return to Raffaele, are the creatures of the idea in the artist's mind. This idea is not inborn; it has come from an intense study. But that study has been of the ideal that can be raised from the positive and the actual into grandeur and beauty. The commonest model becomes full of exquisite suggestions to him who has formed this idea; a Venus of flesh and blood would be vulgarized by the imitation of him who has not.

When asked where he got his models, Guido summoned a common porter from his calling, and drew from a mean original a head of surpassing beauty. It resembled the porter, but idealized the porter to the hero. It was true, but it was not real. There are critics who will tell you that the Boor of Teniers is more true to nature than the Porter of Guido! The

common-place public scarcely understand the ideali-
zing principle, even in art. For high art is an
acquired taste.

V

APTITUDES FOR BUSINESS

Aptitudes for business are indicated by the following
signs:—

  i. Good Line of Fate.

  ii. A vivid and deep Line of Head.

  iii. The straight Line of Head.

  iv. The Line of Head not entangled with the Line
of Life.

  v. Mount of Mercury prominent.

  vi. Branches from the Line of Head to the Mount
of Mercury.

  vii. The length of Fourth Finger above the average.

  viii. Strong first phalanx of the thumb.

  ix. Fingers with second knot and square tips.

  x. Fingers longer than palm.

  xi. The Line of Head forked with one prong going
to the Mount of Mercury.

  xii. The Fate Line going up to the Mount of Mercury.

  xiii. A branch from Fate Line reaching the Mount
of Mercury.

Follow Ford Formula

This is what William C. Richards writes about Henry
Ford: the Last Billionaire:

When Ford had his first blast furnace in mind, experts assured him it was absolutely necessary to have a first heating and then to reheat and remelt the product. That's the way it always had been done.

"Don't believe it", he frowned on these advisers in the steel areas. He told his own men that because it hadn't been done was a good reason the motor company should try it.

Ford told stevenson confidently that it would be quite simple to make castings direct from the ore and save the expense of double melting, and Stevenson jumped on it as proof of Ford's wilfulness and erraticism.

"Who is doing this sort of thing now?" the lawyer asked.

"Nobody".

"And you are going to experiment with Ford Company money to do it, are you? You're going to undertake something nobody has even tried before?"

Ford said he certainly was.

"There wouldn't be any fun for us if we didn't try things people say we can't do", he smiled, broadly.

"At Ford Motor Company expense?"

"That's all I am working for at present—a little fun and to do the most good for the most people."

Ford had a comfortable assurance. He really knew nothing of his competitors or how many there were— that's what he said. He had all he could do to mind his own business. "The minutes spent on other people's business we lose on our own", he put it. Had he given thought to whether he could undersell those competitors he said he never considered? He didn't belong in business if he couldn't, he said blithely. Ford Motor could keep up with competition so long as it worked harder than others did.

It was from C. Harold Wills, chief of manufacturing the Court got the backstage story of Ford Motor. Success was not merely a matter of streams of drive-aways leaving the back door and Ford, doubled up happily by the burden, running out the front hourly to bank another million.

Wills had worked with Ford, in developing the car three years before the incorporation. They had shivered together in an unheated loft and when it got too bad they put on boxing gloves and slugged each other to keep warm. The trade understood what Wills said if it did not always know what Ford was driving at. He put no frosting of sentimental motive on the cake.

So you have got to think hard, work hard and live hard to keep your head above water in the ocean of the business world. Mere signs in the hand are not enough.

VI

CHEMICAL ENGINEERING

Success in Chemistry is shown by short vertical lines on the Mount of Mercury.

The aspiring student, however, should not delimit himself to the Modern Chemistry, because it appears that a Chemistry in ancient times was far more advanced that our own. Thus Bulwer Lytton writes:—

Nor were these studies limited to chemical discovery—in which it is permitted me to say that the greatest marvels upon the organization of physical life seemed wrought by experiments of the vivifying influence of Heat. Mejnour professed to find a link between all intellectual beings in the existence of a certain all-pervading and invisible fluid resembling electricity, yet distinct from the known operations of that mysterious agency—a fluid that connected thought to thought with the rapidity and precision of the modern telegraph, and the influence of this influence, according to Mejnour, extended to the remotest past—that is to say, whenever and wheresoever man has thought. Thus, if the doctrine were true, all human knowledge became attainable through a medium established between the brain of the individual inquirer, and all the farthest and obscurest regions in the universe of ideas.

VII

COMMERCIAL ARTIST

A successful commercial artist is shown by the following signs:—

i. Mounts of Apollo and Mercury predominate.
ii. The Hand is Spatulate.
iii. The Line of Head is straight.
iv. A drooping Line of Head on a Square Hand.
v. An influence Line from the Mount of Apollo edges on the Mount of Mercury.
vi. Fingers are square-tipped.
vii. A whorl between third and fourth fingers gives a person the capacity to commercialize his artistic qualities.

VIII

MUSICIAN

A successful composer of music is indicated by the following signs:—

i. Strong Mount of Mercury.
ii. Square-tipped fingers.
iii. A well-developed Mount of Moon.

With these signs you will not only be a successful musician but also be successful in earning your living as an musician. The trouble with many musicians is that they are not able to earn their living by it.

> At Naples, in the latter half of the last century, a worthy artist named Gaetano Pisani, lived and flourished. He was a musician of great genius, but not of popular reputation; there was in all his compositions something capricious and fantastic, which did not please the taste of the Dilettanti of Naples. He was fond of unfamiliar subjects, into which he introduced airs and symphonies that excited a kind of terror in those who listened . . . Fortunately, or the poor musician might have starved, he was not only a composer, but also an excellent practical performer, especially on the violin, and by that instrument he earned a decent subsistence as one of the orchestra at the Great Theatre of San Carlo.

IX

CRITIC'S HAND

A good critic has the following signs in his hand:—
i. Short well-formed nails.

    ii.   Cross in the Plain of Mars.
   iii.   Predominant Mount of Mercury.
   iv.   Second phalanges of all fingers abnormal.
    v.   Fingers with strong first knots.
   vi.   Soft palm.

"Of all cants", said Laurence Sterne in **Tristram Shandy,** "which are canted in this canting world—though the cant of hypocrites may be the worst—the cant of criticism is the most tormenting."

Criticism has killed many artists and poets, Chatterton being one of them. There are few who appreciate criticism like Victor Hugo: "I had rather be hissed for a good verse than applauded for a bad one."

X

SUCCESSFUL DIPLOMAT

These are the indications of a successful diplomat:—

     i.   Fourth finger pointed.
    ii.   A triangle on the Mount of Mercury.
   iii.   The Line of Fate going to the Mount of Jupiter.
   iv.   The Line of Head sloping.
    v.   Square Hand.
   vi.   Thumb elastic.
  vii.   A well-formed Quadrangle.
 viii.   Life Line deep and vivid.
   ix.   The Line of Heart shallow.

Diplomacy is to do and say
The nastiest thing in the nicest way.

—Isaac Goldberg

XI

INVENTOR

The inventor is indicated by white lines on the Mount of Saturn or white spots on the Line of Head. Other signs are:—

i. A good triangle
ii. Cross in the Quadrangle.
iii. A branch line from the Mount of Luna to the Line of Head.
iv. Almond-shaped hand.
v. Square-tipped nails.

XII

FILM PRODUCER

i. The Line of Extraordinary Dramatic Expression rises from the side of the hand in the vicinity of the Mount of Luna towards the base of the middle finger.
ii. Line of Life and Line of Head separated at the start.
iii. The Line of Head with a fork at the end.
iv. High Mounts of Jupiter, Apollo and Mercury.
v. First phalanx of the thumb very good.
vi. Square fingers with no knots.

XIII

A VISIONARY'S HAND

    i. A cross near the Line of Apollo.
   ii. Line of Intuition islanded.
  iii. Very drooping Line of Head.
   iv. Mounts of Moon, Venus and Saturn prominent.
    v. Thin, elongated palm.
   vi. Long, slender-pointed fingers.

XIV

PUBLIC SPEAKER

    i. Line of Head long, forked and sloping.
   ii. Excellent Line of Heart.
  iii. Mount of Venus very good.
   iv. Fine Mounts of Jupiter and Apollo.
    v. Lines of Life and Head separated at the start.

XV

CONFIDENCE TRICKSTER

    i. Thin soft hand.
   ii. Fingers, long and knotty.
  iii. Mounts of Jupiter and Apollo exaggerated.
   iv. Widely forked Line of Head.

   v. Mount of Mercury predominant.
  vi. Star or Grille on the Mount of Mercury.
 vii. Third Finger above normal in length.
viii. Fourth finger crooked.

XVI

ENGINEER'S HAND

    i. Broad palm.
   ii. Flat Mounts.
  iii. Spatulate Fingers.
  iv. Straight Line of Head.
   v. Mounts of Mars large and fine.
  vi. Scientific markings on the Mount of Mercury.
 vii. Mount of Saturn predominant.
viii. Long knotty fingers.

XVII

WASTER OF INHERITANCE

    i. Line of Fate stopping early.
   ii. Line of Apollo dim or Absent.
  iii. Mount of Apollo poor.
  iv. Sloping Line of Head.
   v. Life Line separated from Head Line at the start.
  vi. Fingers flexible.
 vii. Thumb set very low.
viii. First phalanx of the thumb thrown backwards.

XVIII

FORGER'S HAND

  i. No Mount of Jupiter.
  ii. Line of Head straight and widely forked.
  iii. Mount of Moon heavy.
  iv. Long, slender crooked fingers.
  v. Mount of Mercury exaggerated.
  vi. Mount of Venus and Apollo well-developed.

XIX

GAMBLER'S HAND

  i. A very drooping Line of Head.
  ii. Large Mount of Moon.
  iii. Third Finger equal to the Second Finger.
  iv. Short smooth fingers.
  v. Soft hand.

XX

HAPPY-GO-LUCKY FELLOW

  i. Hand thick and soft.
  ii. Mounts of Jupiter and Venus well-developed.
  iii. Very good Line of Fate.

 iv. Life Line vivid and deep, without breaks.
 v. No worry lines.
 vi. Heart line broad and deep.
 vii. No Girdle of Venus.
 viii. Good travel lines.

XXI

THE EXCELLENT HOUSEWIFE

 i. The Line of Head moderately long.
 ii. Clearly marked Main Lines.
 iii. Hand free from confused branch lines.
 iv. Mounts of Venus and Mercury pronounced.
 v. Long Line of Heart.
 vi. Heart Line starting from Mount of Jupiter.
 vii. Mounts moderate.
 viii. Nails short.
 ix. Fingers square.
 x. First knot of fingers quite marked.
 xi. Palm elastic.
 xii. Palm and fingers even.

XXII

CALL OF IDEALISM

 i. Mounts of Sun and Moon predominant.
 ii. Drooping Line of Head.
 iii. High Mount of Moon.
 iv. Fine Mount of Jupiter.

v. The first finger excellent.
vi. Thin soft hands.
vii. Pointed fingers.

XXIII

CREATIVE WRITER

i. A perfect broad Triangle.
ii. Well-developed Mounts of Moon and Venus.
iii. Mounts of Jupiter and Apollo excellent.
iv. Almond-shaped nails.
v. First phalanx of fingers long.
vi. Soft hands.
vii. Palm smaller than fingers.
viii. Pointed finger tips.

XXIV

RICH INHERITANCE

i. A long sister line to the Line of Head.
ii. Star on the first bracelet of the Rascette.
iii. Cross within the Triangle.
iv. A good Line of Fate rising from the wrist.
v. Line of Fate going to the Mount of Mercury,
vi. A line from the Mount of Moon touching Fate Line.

XXV

OCCULTIST

i. A Triangle on the Mount of Moon.
ii. Drooping Line of Head.
iii. Line of Fate rising from the Mount of Moon.
iv. A fine Triangle.
v. A clear Line of Intuition.
vi. A clear Line of Liver.
vii. Thin and very soft hands.
viii. Short nails.
ix. Short smooth conical fingers.
x. First phalanx of fingers long.
xi. First phalanx of thumb long.
xii. Mounts of Moon and Mercury predominant.
xiii. Mount of Saturn strongly marked.
xiv. Thumb conical.

XXVI

INTELLECTUAL CAREER

i. Excellent lines of Head and Liver.
ii. Long Line of Heart.
iii. Line of Heart slopping.
iv. Line of Heart forked.
v. Sloping Line of Head.
vi. Superb Line of Head.
vii. Mounts of Jupiter, Apollo and Mercury predominant.

    viii. Fingers longer than the palm.
      ix. Fingers conical.
       x. Fingers knotted.

XXVII

JACK OF ALL TRADES

When thumbs are set very low in the hand, the subject indicated is a Jack of all trades—and master of none.

XXVIII

JUDGE'S HAND

    i. Good Head Line.
    ii. Long come fingers.
   iii. A wide Quadrangle.
   iv. Long first phalanx of Mercury finger.
    v. Good Mount of Apollo.
   vi. Straight Jupiter finger.

XXIX

LAWYER'S HAND

    i. Head Line separated from Life Line at the start.
    ii. Line of Head forked at the termination.
   iii. Large Mounts of Mercury and Mars.

  iv. Long second phalanx of the thumb.
   v. Fourth finger predominant.
  vi. Short nails.
 vii. Long straight thumb.
viii. Fingers long and close.
  ix. Straight Head Line.
   x. Flat palm.

XXX

LITERARY SUCCESS

   i. The Line of Apollo very good.
  ii. A cross on the finger of Jupiter.
 iii. A star or white spot on the Mount of Apollo.
 iv. Girdle of Venus good.
  v. Branch of Fate Line going to the Mount of
     Mercury.
 vi. Mounts of Saturn and Apollo well-formed.
 vii. A Line from Rascette going up to the Mount
     of Moon.
viii. Drooping Line of Head.
  ix. Line of Head forked at the termination.
   x. White dots on the line of Head.
  xi. Long first and fourth fingers.
 xii. Fingers conical.
xiii. Mounts of Mercury and Apollo predominant.

XXXI

DANGEROUS MADNESS

  i. Mounts of Moon and Mars exaggerated.
 ii. All lines in the palm very red.

iii. The Line of Life of livid colour.
iv. The sign of Mars on the Mount of Moon.
v. The sign of Moon on the Mount of Mars.

XXXII

MATHEMATICIAN'S HAND

i. Mounts of Apollo and Moon absent.
ii. Very straight Line of Head.
iii. Second phalanges of fingers and thumb abnormal.
iv. Mounts of Saturn and Mercury predominant.
v. The Fourth Finger above normal.
vi. Fingers long and knotted.
vii. Dry hard palm.

XXXIII

MECHANICAL ENGINEER

i. Straight Line of Head.
ii. Mount of Mercury thrown towards the Mount of Apollo.
iii. Palm longer than fingers.
iv. Fingers with square tips.
v. Second knots of fingers marked.

XXXIV

MILITARY CAREER

    i.   The Mount of Mercury leaning towards the upper Mount of Mars.
   ii.   A star or triangle on either Mount of Mars.
  iii.   A triangle between the Line of Fate and the Line of Life.
  iv.   One deep line on third phalanx of second finger.
    v.   Triangle on Upper Mount of Mars.
  vi.   Triangle in the Plain of Mars.
 vii.   Only principal lines indicate on the hand.
viii.   Strong Mounts of Venus and Jupiter.
  ix.   Palm longer than fingers.
    x.   Fingers with square tips.
  xi.   Mounts and the Plain of Mars predominant.

XXXV

NAVAL PROFESSION

    i.   Large knotted fingers.
   ii.   A large Mount of Moon.
  iii.   Mount of Moon much lined.
  iv.   Fine Mounts and Plain of Mars.
    v.   Large first phalanx of the thumb.
  vi.   Drooping Line of Head.
 vii.   Line of Head separated at the start from the Line of Life.

XXXVI

OPERA SINGER

i. Palm larger than the fingers.
ii. Fingers with conical tips.
iii. Lines of Life and Head widely separated at the start.
iv. Line of Head forked at the termination.

XXXVII

SUCCESSFUL PAINTER

i. Conically tipped fingers.
ii. Strong Mount of Venus.
iii. Mount of Apollo excellent.
iv. Strong Mount of Moon.
v. Drooping Line of Head.
vi. Soft hands.

XXXVIII

PHILOSOPHER'S HAND

i. A prominence on the first finger outside the topmost joint.
ii. Very long knotted fingers.
iii. Thin hard palm.

iv. Fingers spatulate.
v. Finger tips conical.
vi. Good lines of Head and Heart.

XXXIX

POET'S HAND

i. Pointed fingers.
ii. Line of Heart chained.
iii. Line of Fate islanded.
iv. Drooping Lines of Head.
v. Mounts of Apollo, Moon and Venus prominent.
vi. Thin soft palm.
vii. Long thin first phalanx of the thumb.

XL

POLITICIAN'S HAND

i. The Line of Head drooping.
ii. Upper Mount of Mars much lined.
iii. Exaggerated Mount of Jupiter.
iv. Mount of Mercury insignificant.
v. Mount of Mercury heavily marked.

XLI

PRIEST'S HAND

i. Cross in the Quadrangle.
ii. Good Lines of Head and Heart.

  iii. Mount of Venus moderate.
  iv. Short nails.
   v. Pointed first finger.
  vi. A good Apollo finger.
 vii. Long fingers.
viii. Conic Finger of Jupiter.
  ix. First phalanx of Mercury finger long.
   x. Mount of Venus good.
  xi. Luna well-developed.
 xii. Straight Jupiter finger.

XLII

PSYCHIC HAND

   i. Almond-shaped hands.
  ii. Long, narrow hands.
 iii. Slender tapering fingers.
 iv. Long almond-shaped nails.

XLIII

PUBLIC HONOURS

   i. Triangle on the Mount of Mercury.
  ii. A star on the first joint of the first finger.
 iii. A star on the Mount of Jupiter.

XLIV

SCHOLAR'S HAND

  i. Good Head Line.
 ii. Good Mount of Luna.

iii. Short nails.
iv. A long first phalanx of Mercury finger.
v. Well-developed conic finger of Jupiter.

XLV

SCIENTIST'S HAND

i. Fourth Finger as long as the second.
ii. A triangle on the Line of Head.
iii. White dots on the Line of Head.

XLVI

SCULPTOR'S HAND

i. Square-tipped fingers.
ii. Mount of Apollo well-developed.
iii. Mount of Venus strong.
iv. Strong Mount of Moon.
v. Head Line drooping slightly.
vi. Soft hands.

XLVII

SEERS, SAINTS & SAGES

i. Line of Intuition.
ii. Mystic cross.
iii. High Mount of Moon.
iv. Pointed Smooth Fingers.

P. E.—9

    v.   Transparent hand.
   vi.   Almond-shaped nails.

XLVIII

SPECULATOR'S HAND

    i.   A sloping Line of Head.
   ii.   The third finger almost as long as the second.

XLIX

SPORTSMAN'S HAND

    i.   Mounts very low.
   ii.   Only main lines indicated.
  iii.   No worry lines.
   iv.   Large hard hand.
    v.   Spatulate finger tips.
   vi.   Third finger longer than normal.
  vii.   Lines of Life and Head separated at the start.

L

SURGEON'S HAND

    i.   Long fingers.
   ii.   Second knot developed in all hands.
  iii.   Firm palm.
   iv.   Head Line clear and deep.
    v.   "Science Lines" on Mercury Finger.

Chapter Thirty-Two

THE CROWNING CAREERS

Uneasy lies the head that wears a crown.

—Shakespeare

It is the prerogative of great men only to have great defects.
—La Rouchefoucauld

The nearer we come to great men, the more clearly we see that they are only men. They rarely seem great to their valets.

—La Bruyere

So ne are born great, some achieve greatness, and some have greatness thrust upon them.

—Shakespeare

The hand of a saint and a sinner, a philosopher and a fool, a king and a clown, is not very much apart. If Valmiki the Highwayman could become overnight Valmiki the High Priest, it is just due to a little twist here and there in the lines. And these are the little turns and twists of lines which are the hardest the read. That is why many men whom we give a very good certificate do not live up to our pretensions and predictions. On the contrary, many people whom we divine to be doomed turn out to be delightful divine or at any rate divinely delightful, thereby falsifying the palmist. All this shows that the lines of a hand cannot be read by one who runs, and all pavement palmists must be dumped in this category. Palm-reading is a very serious study, and it should heed days if not weeks and months.

"In my travels around the world as a newspaperman
and writer", says Josef Ranald, "I interviewed thousands
of world-famous personalities, outstanding in every line
of endeavour. What most amazed me was finding in the
hands of these celebrated people certain lines definitely
indicating their individual talents."

                                     I

                GREAT GOLDEN GRETA GARBO!

Age cannot wither her, nor custom stale
Her infinite variety.

                              —Shakespeare

What Shakespeare said about Cleopatra is true of Greta
Garbo. Age cannot wither her! And custom cannot
stale her infinite variety! Actresses come and go, but
Greta Garbo goes on forever!

Greta Garbo has, what Josaf Ranald calls, "The Line
of Emotional Moods". It encircles the base of her first
finger. It is significant of the power expressing emotions
in either dramatic or musical productions.

Greta Garbo was born in Stockholm in 1906.   Her
real name is Greta Gustafson. She began her career as
a stage dancer. It was only when she came to the United
States in 1925 that she attained instant success on the
screen. Therefore, her travel lines—"Lines of No Return"—are important. The flexibility of her thumb is indicative of her exotic and fascinating personality.

II

WOODROW WILSON

Professor Woodrow Wilson rose to be the President of the United States of America—the first and the last professor to occupy the White House. A contemporary palmist wrote about him:—

> "The thumb of President Wilson's hand is low set, well-developed and well-formed at the tip. This gives fine capacity for thought and action, indicating a genius for knowing when to go ahead backed by sound judgment.
>
> "The finger tips denote intellectuality and mental powers, combined with a vivid imagination. Well-spaced and evenly set on the palm, the fingers denote independence of thought and action. These are the type of fingers that show much capacity for detail, in as much as their possessors are always interested in processes by which results are obtained."

III

FRANKLIN D. ROOSEVELT

President Roosevelt, who became President of America four times, had a hand which showed that he was a great lover of land and the people. Through the force of his Heart Line, which started below the first finger, denoted a calm, evenly balanced unemotional nature and the quality of drawing the people to him. Alice Denton Jennings thus writes about this great man's hand:—

"The Fate Line, starting as it does, low on the Mount of the Moon to the side of the hand, destined President Roosevelt to lead public life. This line, traversing the hand, as it does in a straight unbroken line, denotes his unusual and outstanding public success.

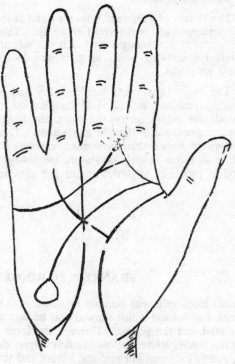

Woodrow Wilson

"The Head Line, gently sloping, taken in combination with an unusually well-marked Intuition Line, gives the power of vision combined with the power of execution, putting through into tangible form, and presenting it in such a manner as to make it clear to others. Ending in a fork, it doubles the powers of these faculties.

"The well-developed Mount of Mercury gives wit, honour and great recuperative powers."

IV

MAHATMA GANDHI

Josaf Ronald writes thus about the hands of Mahatma Gandhi:—

"The Triangle of Wisdom is formed in the centre of the hand by the intersection of three lines revealing an inner strength and wisdom which borders on the superhuman. And that wisdom and that moral strength, which this triangle indicates, has shown to the world many times over the great Mahatma or Great Soul of India. His is the wisdom of passive resistance and the strength to carry it out, as he struggles valiantly for the independence of his people, and obliteration of the caste system that made millions of untouchables, outcastes forced to a life of abject misery. Time and again the British authorities have thrown him into prison for his demonstrations, but still they have grudgingly been grateful to the Mahatma for his advocacy and enforcement of non-violent resistance. The power which he has attained has resulted from his extraordinary self-effacement. He holds that peace and love will solve all problems, and he is resolved to do all in his power to make love a practical force in this world. His hand clearly shows the lines of imperial conquests, yet his indomitable will directs his destiny and he cares only for the power necessary to relieve his millions of followers from the inhuman caste system."

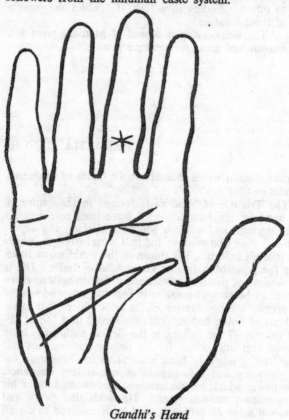

Gandhi's Hand

V

EUGENE SANDOW

Eugene Sandow was known as "The Strongest Man". He had a thick palm, almost square horizontally and vertically. The lines were few and deep, showing a clear-

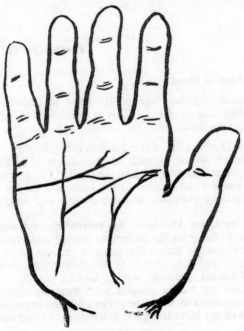

Eugene Sandow

cut destiny without any mental confusion. His thumb was strong and showed his strong determination in whatever he was called upon to do. His head line was slightly away from the Life Line at the start, thus showing independence of character that is always reasonable and open to take better advice.

VI

CHEIRO'S HAND

Double Line of Head

The most important sign on the hand of Cheiro was his Double Line of Head. This is what Cheiro writes about his own hand:—

"A Double Line of Head is very rarely found. The character shown by each of these Lines of Head is in apparent contradiction to the other. For example, the lower closely joined to the Line of Life denotes a mentality extremely sensitive, artistic and imaginative.

"The upper line gives the reverse characteristics, namely, rising on the Mount of Jupiter and running nearly straight across the palm, it denotes self-confidence, ambition, power to dominate others and a level-headed, practical way of looking at life.

"One can hardly imagine such mentally opposite characteristics in the same person, but the impression given of my hand is a good illustration of these statements.

"On my left hand there is no sign whatever of any upper Head Line –there is only the lower line to be

seen; and is a curious fact that the appearance of
the Upper Head Line on my right hand only com-
menced to be noticeable when I was about thirty
years of age.

"At this point of my life, circumstances brought me
before the world as a lecturer and public speaker.
This forced me to make a supreme effort to overcome
my supreme sensitiveness as shown by the lower Head
Line, with the result that the upper line began to deve-
lop and in a few years became the dominant one on
my right hand.

"I have also stated that in cases where double Line
of Head is found, persons who possess these lines
are inclined to live what are called double lives of
one form or another.   ...

"In my own particular case this has been remark-
ably true, for more than fifty years one section of
the public only knew me under my own name.

"I can further state here that due to the influence
of the more sensitive side of my nature, for many
years I gave vent to my feelings by writing poetry,
both sentimental and religious, while at the same
time, the other side was engaged in appearing as a
lecturer on public platforms. as war correspondent,
and later, as editor of newspapers in London and
Paris."

VII

JULIUS CEASAR

Julius Ceasar himself was a palmist. It is related by
Josephius, the historian, that Julius Ceasar was so much
well-versed in Palmistry that "one day a so-called son of

Herod had audience with him, and he at once detected the imposter because his hand was destitute of all marks of royalty."

In the palm of Julius Ceasar, the Line of Head was rising towards the Line of Heart; and this was why he suffered from fainting fits, and also that his head was governed by the heart. He was so good at heart and so poor in head that his assassinators duped him at the very time of his assassination. He was too good to think that anybody would kill him, particularly Brutus to whom he was specially favourable, and his last words were **Et tu Brute!** (You too Brutus!). He was so shocked to see Brutus among the murderers that he immediately collapsed without making the slightest effort for self-defence. It was all because his head was under the control of his heart.

VIII

WINSTON CHURCHILL

According to Rita Van Alen, "Winston Churchill's thumbs reveal a personally generous side of his nature". His familiar "Thumb up", so well-known to the world, became V for Victory, and helped to stiffen the backbone of a war-worn world.

IX

GEORGE BERNARD SHAW

George Bernard Shaw had the line of intellect and wit. The Line of Intellect and Wit rises from the centre of the palm upwards to the base of the third finger. It denotes an original and sparkling personality. This line is very rarely seen.

X

HAMLET

Dangerous morbidness and a tendency to suicide, of to-be-or-not-to-be type of Hamlet, the Prince of Denmark, was indicated by an exaggerated Mount of Saturn.

XI

MADAME CURIE

Madame Curie, the most famous woman scientist of the world, had the Line of Intuition which helped her to discover radium.

The Line of Intuition starts below the fourth finger on the side of the hand and takes a course in a semicircular form, down the palm, denoting a highly intuitive mind and enabling its possessor to solve sometimes baffling mysteries, where the keenest minds have been vainly searching for a solution.

XII

NAPOLEON BONAPARTE

The first finger of Napoleon was equal to the second. Wherever this sign occurs, it is called "Napoleon's Index".

It is an indication of great political ambition, military glory and boundless love of wealth and power.

XIII

KING SOLOMON

King Solomon had a strange ring, having its source between the fingers of Jupiter and Saturn. It ended near the start of the Life Line. It was a great mark of occult and mysticism which made him not only a great king but also a great magician and spiritualist.

XIV

HELEN KELLER

Stars of Unusual Faculties are found on the tips of the fingers of Helen Keller, the blind international leader. These are witnesses of an acute sense of touch. Little wonder, Helen Keller can hear, see and read through her finger-tips. Struck incurably deaf, dumb and blind at the age of nineteenth months, she has overcome all her handicaps. She is an author, lecturer, educationist and international tourist. She also visited India in 1955.

XV

HENRY FORD

Father William Ford had remarked pessimistically to a friend, "John and William (Henry's brothers) are all right but Henry worries me. He doesn't seem to settle down to anything and I don't know what will become of him."

Henry Ford had a square hand, strong thumb, and a sloping Line of Head, which enabled him to combine great imagination with a strong practical sense and independent outlook. He had a cross in the Quadrangle which gave him deep, hidden, occult powers about the mysteries of the unknown. "He told his associates", says William C. Richards, "he felt there was nothing in the world he had not seen in a previous life."

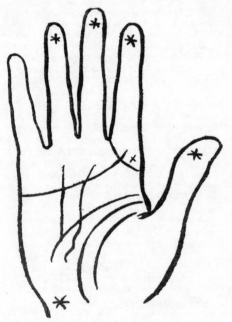

Hellen Keller

XVI

JOHN CAREY

John Carey, the great footballer, had Ring of Saturn showing moodiness, Heart Line reaching Mount of Jupiter showing ambition, Line of Liver showing health delicacy, straight Head Line showing quickness of thought.

Chapter Thirty-Three

GOLDEN GUIDE TO COSY CAREERS

These traits govern the hand according to the proportion in
which they exist, and they must be considered to that extent.
—Henry Frith
"Practical Palmistry"

The signs and symbols of Palmistry must not be blindly read and blindly interpreted. These must not be cut
off from the great principles of Mysticism, Occult, Magic,
Psychology and Hypnotism.

Great harm can be done by reading a book of Palmistry
as you read a book of Mathematics or a Law Journal.
There is no Law-journalism about Palmistry, nothing of
the mathematical incorrigibility. So proceed with caution.

I

AVOID EVIL INTERPRETATIONS

Concentrate on what is good in the hand rather than
what is evil. Lay more emphasis on points of strength
in a character rather than its weaknesses. By stressing
strong points, you bring them to the fore and these help
to suppress evil indications in the hand. By laying too
much stress on evils you see in a hand, you destroy the
little good that might be therein. Remember, a little
strong good can kill a great deal of weak evil.

"What is evil?" said Nietzsche.   "Whatever springs from weakness."

There is much more hope for mentally strong bad characters than mentally weak priests, politicians or professors.

II

STRESS LESSER EVILS

Always emphasize lesser rather than greater evils in a hand. If a man is going to fall ill or die at a certain age, tell him of illness and how to protect against it. Do not tell him of death.

"Of two evils", says Erasmus, "choose the least."

III

EVIL NEVER CONQUERS

One good point is more powerful than ten bad points. Gradually a tiny candle-light disperses oceans of darkness. Remember, as Joseph Roux said, "Evil often triumphs, but never conquers." Good alone conquers evil. Therefore, if a man has one good point against ten bad points, you must guide him as to how that one point can vanquish his ten defects.

IV

THERE IS NO EVIL IN THE WORLD

Remember that every evil is an agent for good. If a person is physically weak, he is likely to be intellectually strong. If R. L. Stevenson were not consumptive, he would not have been a great writer. So always look for good behind an evil. There never was an evil unaccompanied by some good results. If a person has no money after fifty, it is because he does not need any money, because he dies, turns a yogi or his children look after him.

Remember what Voltaire said, "Everything is for the best in this best of all possible worlds."

V

VALUATE PROPERLY

Try to give a right character and career value to all those whose hands you have the opportunity to see. Most of the palmists are either too flattering or condemnatory according to the money-value of the person concerned. Try to be objective in your valuations notwithstanding the fees offered to you.

"We are valued", says Marie Ebner Eschenbach, "either too highly or not high enough; we are never taken at our real worth."

VI

WANTED WORSHIP VALUES

Maintain a worshipful attitude towards Plamistry and towards the objects of your study. Remember that Palmistry is a realm "where man is the holiest of holies". When we try to reduce Palmistry to the science of a charlatan whose only business is fee-taking, Palmistry vanishes. It becomes another form of quackery like Medicine which, like Palmistry, was once a Holy Science.

"It is only when men begin to worship", says Calvin Coolidge, "that they begin to grow."

VII

DO NOT OVERDO THE DREADS

If you notice an unpleasant incident in the life of a person, express it in a manner to caution him and protect him against it instead of frightening him. When the hand shows a danger, it shows also the means and methods to ward it off. You must stress the latter rather than the former.

Beware of the palmists who find a sadistic pleasure in frightening you about your future without offering adequate safeguards.

"The lion is not so fierce", as Herbert said, "as they paint him."

VIII

LESSON IN HUMILITY

"Be humble" was the message of Gandhiji. No true understanding of life and its laws is possible without humility.

Learn humility and teach humility.

As Barrie said in **Little Minister,** "Life is a long lesson in humility."

There is no place for pride of knowledge or prediction in the theory and practice of Palmistry. In order to understand, you must stand under!

IX

LIFE IS A JIGSAW PUZZLE

If you look carefully at the hands of anybody, you will find it a map fraught with confused lines.

As an anonymous writer has said, "Life is a jig saw puzzle with most of the pieces missing."

A good palmist must supply these missing pieces imaginatively in order to construct a complete picture of the subject's life.

X

A USELESS LIFE IS EARLY DEATH

Do not see how short is the life of a man but also how usefully he lives. Those who have very short lives usually are very worthwhile people. As the Roman saying goes, "Those whom gods love, they die young."

On the contrary, men with long lives may be leading a futile humdrum existence. They are as good as dead. As Goethe said, "A useless life is an early death."

XI

LIFE'S A FAIRY TALE

If you study the lines carefully, you will find that the life of even the humblest man is a fairy tale. You will find much of interest and delight. Every person is a kingdom to himself.

"Every man's life is a fairy-tale written by God's fingers", said Hans Christian Andersen.

As a palmist, you should show your subject the path to the fairyland that is within and without him. If you can't put him on the highway to the fairyland of his career and character, you are indeed a failure.

XII

DON'T PREDICT DEATH BY DISEASE

If a person is likely to suffer from a certain disease, or is now suffering, don't frighten him to death. Rather show him the path to avoid the same.

As Erasmus said, "No one is to be despaired of as long as he breathes."

XIII

LIVE FAST AND DIE EARLY

People today live fast and die early. They want to live fast and die early. Nobody is interested in a long

mournful life. Tell people not how long they will live,
but how much they can be happy in the present context
of their lives. As Edna St. Vincent Milay wrote in **Figs
from Thistles:**

> My candle burns at both ends;
> It will not last the night;
> But, ah, my foes, and, oh, my friends—
> It gives a lovely light.

As Tagore said: "Let your life lightly dance on the
edges of Time like dew on the tip of a leaf."

BIBLIOGRAPHY

Dennis Barry Jackson—**The Modern Palmist**

Subhash J. Rele—an article in **Sunday Standard**

Cheiro—**World Predictions**

Balzac—**Le Cousin Pons**

Alice Denton Jennings—**Your Hand Tells All**

Rita Van Alen—**You and Your Hand**

William C. Benham—**The Laws of Scientific Hand Reading**

Bulwer Lytton—**Zanoni**

Jagat S. Bright—**Dictionary of Palmistry**

Comte C. de Saint-Germain—**Practical Palmistry**

Adrian Desbarrolles—**L. Anneau de Venus**

Nelie Simmons Meier—**The Lion Paws**

William C. Richards—**Henry Ford: the Last Billionaire**

Henry Frith—**Practical Palmistry**

Cheiro—**Language of the Hand**

F. R. Cherill—article in **Prediction**

d'Arpentigny—**Palmistry**

Martini—**Palmistry**

Mercury—**Palmistry**

Josef Ronald—**Your Hands**